EVALUATING VIEWPOINTS:
CRITICAL THINKING IN
UNITED STATES HISTORY SERIES

TEACHER'S GUIDE

BOOK ONE
COLONIES
TO
CONSTITUTION

KEVIN O'REILLY

SERIES TITLES
BOOK 1–COLONIES TO CONSTITUTION
BOOK 2–NEW REPUBLIC TO CIVIL WAR
BOOK 3–RECONSTRUCTION TO PROGRESSIVISM
BOOK 4–SPANISH-AMERICAN WAR TO VIETNAM WAR

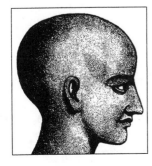
© 1990, 1983
CRITICAL THINKING BOOKS & SOFTWARE
(formerly Midwest Publications)
P.O. Box 448 • Pacific Grove • CA 93950-0448
Phone 800-458-4849 • FAX 831-393-3277 • www.criticalthinking.com
ISBN 0-89455-414-X
Printed in the United States of America

TABLE OF CONTENTS

ABOUT THE AUTHOR

Kevin O'Reilly is a social studies teacher at Hamilton-Wenham Regional High School in Massachusetts. He was named by *Time* magazine and the National Council for the Social Studies as the 1986 Outstanding Social Studies Teacher in the United States. In addition to these four volumes on Critical Thinking in United States History, Mr. O'Reilly is the coauthor of *Critical Viewing: Stimulant to Critical Thinking* (also published by Midwest Publications/Critical Thinking Press & Software) and the author of "Escalation," the computer simulation on the Vietnam War (Kevin O'Reilly, 6 Mason Street, Beverly, MA 01915). Mr. O'Reilly, who has a Master of Arts Degree in History, is an editor of the *New England Journal of History*. He conducts workshops throughout the United States on critical thinking, critical viewing, and decision making.

ACKNOWLEDGEMENTS

I would like to thank Richard Trask of the Danvers Archival Center for his suggestions on the Salem Witch Trials (Lesson 10); Bob Swartz of the University of Massachusetts at Boston for his ideas on teaching specific thinking skills, especially cause and effect and generalization; William Payne, a history teacher at Moreno Valley High School in California, for his questions to test value claims; Dick Aieta, Vincent Bucci, Vicki Krupp, Ken Portnoy, Alice Schlossberg, and Ann Tassanari of the social studies department at Hamilton-Wenham for their ideas and support—we've shared and tried out a lot of ideas for teaching history; and my wife Lynn for her love, patience, and support.

INTRODUCTION

Overview of This Section

This teacher's guide contains an introduction, reproducible lessons to introduce each skill covered in the series, suggested teaching strategies and answers for each lesson in the student text, and test questions. The introduction includes:

1. an introduction to the process of critical thinking;

2. a rationale for the series;

3. a description of the role of the teacher, including an overview of the *Teacher's Guide*, suggestions for classroom methods for teaching critical thinking in history, and various suggestions for evaluating student progress;

4. a description of the role of the student, including an overview of the student text;

5. a chart of the scope and sequences of skills developed in this text;

6. a bibliography of sources on critical thinking.

What Is Critical Thinking?

For the purposes of this series, critical thinking is *judging* the worth of claims or arguments. It involves judgment, assessment, evaluation. One author calls critical thinking "reasoned judgment." The critical thinker has a healthy skepticism and asks probing questions; the non-critical thinker is likely to jump to conclusions and believe whatever is claimed.

Critical thinking is not the same as creative thinking, brainstorming, problem solving, decision making, conceptualizing, or Bloom's taxonomy—although it is involved in the judgment phase of problem solving and decision making. Neither is it the same as asking students to compare and contrast or to categorize—for those activities do not require students to evaluate the comparisons made or categories delineated.

Only level six (evaluation) of Bloom's taxonomy involves critical thinking. Level four (analysis) is so important to evaluation of arguments, however, that some of these skills are also directly taught in these books.

The following analysis and evaluation skills are included in the series.

> **— Analysis Skills —**
>
> - Differentiating between conclusions and reasons
> - Identifying types of reasoning
> - Identifying sources of information
> - Classifying parts of an argument based on cue words, value words, emotional words, and change-of-direction words
> - Identifying assumptions and value judgments
>
> **— Evaluation Skills —**
>
> - Evaluating the relevance of reasons to conclusions
> - Evaluating types of reasoning
> - Evaluating sources
> - Evaluating assumptions and value judgments

Overall, then, the critical thinker asks, "Why should I believe this?" and offers reasoned judgments in answer to that question. These books are meant to arm students with the critical-thinking skills necessary to make reasoned judgments, to prod them into asking questions, and to give them the confidence both to ask questions and to offer judgments.

About This Series

This four-volume series, *Evaluating Viewpoints: Critical Thinking in United States History*, is intended to improve critical thinking through evaluation of conflicting viewpoints of United States history. The books are chronological, each covering a particular time period.

Book 1: Colonies Through Constitution (1492–1789)

Book 2: New Republic Through Civil War (1790–1865)

Book 3: Reconstruction Through Progressivism (1865–1914)

Book 4: Spanish-American War Through Vietnam War (1900–1980)

There is not, however, chronological coverage within each book. Each lesson is a self-contained problem that can be "plugged in" at any point in a corresponding history unit. These books are thus meant to supplement other curriculum materials, not to be the sole text for a course.

As mentioned in the introduction of the student text, the root word of history is *story*. In this series, emphasis is on helping students see that the "story" of history can be told different ways and that values, attitudes, perceptions, and selection all shape the way people see the past. These books are intended to show students that historical subject matter is not some unchanging, agreed upon, and complete subject to be memorized, but rather is changing, selective, fragmentary, and open to interpretation.

The target of this series is understanding, not memorizing. Studies in cognitive psychology indicate that memorization lasts only a short time. Focusing on problems, thinking, and understanding helps students remember the content of history much longer.

The Role of the Teacher
About the Teacher's Guide

The *Teacher's Guide* contains:

1. an introduction to the series;
2. reproducible worksheets for introducing each skill;
3. objectives, teaching ideas, and suggested answers for each lesson;
4. possible test questions and suggested answers.

Twelve skill worksheets are included in the *Teacher's Guide* for each book in the series. These can be used to promote a questioning attitude (Worksheet A), introduce particular skills (Worksheets B–J), or serve as general worksheets for evaluating any film or written argument (Worksheets K–L). The teaching ideas and the suggested answers are intended as guidance for the teacher, not as rigid lesson plans or right answers. The emphasis is on thinking, not on "correct" answers.

A key element in the emphasis on teaching, practicing, and repeating critical thinking skills is the "Scope and Sequence of Skills" chart on pages 10–11. Once you have decided which skills to teach, this chart will serve as a quick reference to their location in each book and to help you select appropriate lessons for practice and repetition. Values are included under "Assumptions" in the scope-and-sequence chart, since they are a kind of assumption about the way the world should be. Those lessons focusing on values are marked with a "v".

Some skills are not represented on the scope-and-sequence chart. Although these skills are not **explicitly** taught in any lesson in the book, they are a part of many of the problem lessons. For example, finding the main idea is an important part of evaluating the interpretations in the book. The importance of using key words for encoding parts of arguments is also a part of many problem lessons, but is never explicitly taught in any specific lesson. For further information on critical thinking, refer to the Bibliography of Critical Thinking Sources on page 12 in this book.

Classroom Methods for Teaching Critical Thinking in History

Unlike other anthologies of opposing viewpoints, this series focuses on how to analyze and evaluate arguments. In improving athletic performance, coaches know that a systematic approach works best. Skills must be broken down and their components explained; the athlete has to try the skill with the guidance of the coach; the athlete must repeatedly practice the skill; and, finally, the skills must be applied in the athletic contest. This same method is used in these books to teach skills of critical thinking. Each skill is broken down and explained in the "Guide to Critical Thinking"; with the guidance of the teacher and/or other students, the student tries the skill on worksheets; additional worksheets provide practice as the student repeats the skill; and, finally, the student applies the skill to new opposing-viewpoint problems. This pattern of skill instruction is outlined below.

Pattern of Skill Instruction

1. INITIAL PROBLEM

In the books in this series, students are confronted with a historical problem from the student text. Since the problem consists of opposing viewpoints, students are forced to evaluate the viewpoints to arrive at a conclusion. This raises the need to learn to think critically in deciding which viewpoint to believe.

2. FAMILIAR EXAMPLE

The teacher gives the class an everyday problem, either from the "Guide to Critical Thinking" or an introductory worksheet, on the skill involved in step 1. Familiar examples make it easier for students to learn the skill.

3. METACOGNITION

This step offers direct teaching of analysis and/or evaluation skills. As the class discusses answers to the familiar problem in step 2, they discuss how class members arrived at their answers. The focus here is on *metacognition*—thinking about thinking, not about the content of the problem—and the components are taught directly. What is involved in performing the skill? What are the steps in the skill? What are the criteria for evaluation? A diagram of the steps or criteria is then posted in the classroom and/or drawn in the "skills" section of students' notebooks. Ideally, the students, guided by the teacher, will identify the components of the skill; those the class cannot identify can be taught directly by the teacher using the "Guide to Critical Thinking."

4. GUIDED PRACTICE

The students are referred back to the historical problem in step 1 and directed to discuss its evaluation in light of the skill they have learned. The students employ the skill on the problem and on worksheets with the guidance of the teacher and other students.

5. MASTERY

Students repeatedly practice the skill on additional worksheets and in class discussions.

6. EXTENSION

As the course progresses, students extend the skill as they apply it to new historical problems.

Class Discussions

From this emphasis on specific critical thinking skills, it can be seen that class discussions of the opposing viewpoints presented in the books are not to be free-for-alls, where all opinions are equally good. Students are expected to employ the skills learned in previous classes, to question assertions made by their classmates, and to defend their own assertions with evidence and reasons. This is a far cry from an emphasis on right answers. In this series, the emphasis is on good thinking, not on right answers.

Adaptation

Obviously, some of the lessons in this text are more difficult than others. Teachers can make easy lessons more challenging by eliminating step-by-step questions or worksheets or by making students produce their own examples to illustrate particular skills. Lessons that are too difficult for some classes can be made easier by doing only a portion of the lesson, by focusing on only a single skill, or by giving students the step-by-step worksheet on the topic. Refer to teaching suggestions on specific lessons for further guidance in the difficulty level of each lesson within this book.

Using the "Guide to Critical Thinking"

The "Guide to Critical Thinking," the first unit in each student text, is meant to help teachers with the direct instruction of key elements of the various critical thinking skills. These key skills are summarized in the chart on pages 10–11.

Although the Guide touches on numerous skills related to the evaluation of interpretations or arguments, it focuses on four of these skills: evaluation of evidence, evaluation of cause-and-effect reasoning, evaluation of comparison reasoning (analogy), and evaluation of generalizations. A grasp of these four argument components is an enormous help in the students' ability to think critically.

The section on *evidence* emphasizes the idea of sources of information. Rather than distinguishing between evidence, which has a source, and information, which provides no source, students are simply instructed to ask, "Is there a source?" whenever they encounter information in support of a claim. If not, they are to note that weakness. If yes, they are to evaluate it. Introductory Worksheet B (pp. 31–32 in this book) provides a concrete problem for determining and evaluating evidence.

In the section on *reasoning*, it is again important to note that students are not only taught to identify the type of reasoning but also to evaluate it. It is not enough that a student says, "This is a cause-and-effect argument." The student must also say whether it is a strong or weak cause-and-effect argument and give reasons for saying so. A concrete problem for introducing cause-and-effect reasoning can be found in the teaching ideas for Introductory Worksheet E (pp. 37–38 in this book).

The section on *evaluating comparisons* (analogies) is not the same as the activity of compare and contrast. This critical thinking skill focuses on evaluating comparison arguments, or what is sometimes called analogic reasoning. For example, asking students to compare and contrast the fighting in Nicaragua in the 1980s with the Vietnam War is very different from asking them to evaluate the argument "The United States should not be involved in fighting in Nicaragua because it will turn into another Vietnam." Although both assignments involve basic knowledge of the two situations, the second assignment requires students to identify the type of reasoning used and to implement comparison and contrast without being cued to do so (as in the first assignment). A concrete problem for introducing comparison reasoning is in the teaching ideas for Introductory Worksheet F (pp. 39–40 in this book).

The term *generalization*, rather than *sample reasoning*, is used for this skill. Use the pizza example on page 8 of the student book as a concrete problem for introducing generalizations. Ask "Suppose you bit into a pizza and the bite was cold. What might you conclude about the pizza?" The strength of a generalization can be determined by asking, "How large and representative is the sample?" Some people, however, believe that randomness is better than representativeness as a method for achieving an accurate sample. In any event, you might want to mention to your students that randomness is also a commonly accepted method of sampling.

Fallacies, although included with each type of reasoning, are not emphasized either in the Guide or in the lessons. Simply teaching students a few questions to ask (and the willingness to ask them) within several broad areas of reasoning will usually be more helpful than teaching them a larger number of fallacies and having them try to fit real arguments into one of these fallacies.

Several points emphasized in the ARMEAR model on page 18 in the student text are not emphasized elsewhere in the Guide. One such point is questions about the author (A); the second is relevant information (R). Students should be taught to bring any information that might be relevant to bear on the topic. They may, of course, have difficulty determining what is relevant. Additionally, they are not in the habit of seeing the relevance of one topic to another. To encourage the habit of thinking about what might be relevant to a historical problem, a number of lessons include relevant information sheets. Students who don't use the sheets can't do a complete analysis of the arguments. Encouraging this habit of calling on what they know helps students view history as a fund of knowledge to be drawn upon to help provide perspective on other, similar issues. History thereby becomes more meaningful.

Skill Transfer

Many of the worksheets contain both everyday and historic argument examples. This mixture is intended to promote transfer of the skills learned into other areas of the students' lives. Teachers can facilitate this transfer of critical thinking skills learned in history class to other subject areas by having students debate topics then analyze the reasoning they used in the debate. When students realize that they use the same reasoning elements in their own thinking, they are more likely to transfer them into other areas of their life. Another important method for promoting skill transfer is to listen carefully to student chatter before class starts. If you can ask a question on the use of a particular type of reasoning on a topic heard in a student conversation, you will connect the skill learned in history to the students' everyday lives.

Evaluation

Test questions are provided at the end of this teacher's guide, and the many problem sheets in the student text provide even more possible test questions. Of course, teachers should consider the viewpoints in the longer problems for essay assignments. These can be evaluation essays, such as "Evaluate Historian A's argument on immigration. In your essay identify and evaluate two pieces of evidence and two types of reasoning."

WRITING AND THINKING

Writing skills are an important part of this curriculum, and students should also be held accountable for their critical thinking skills when they write any essay assignment. An example student assignment might be, "Write a minimum 250-word essay on the main cause of the American Revolution. In your essay you are to show what makes a strong cause, support your case with one piece of evidence, and explain why this is strong evidence." Students must learn how to construct strong arguments in addition to evaluating the arguments made by others.

Overview of Book 1

Book 1 is comprised of the "Guide to Critical Thinking" (Unit 1) and twenty-nine lessons divided into three units. Lessons 1–10 are in the Colonies Unit; Lessons 11–19 in the American Revolution Unit; and Lessons 20–29 in the Constitution Unit. The table of contents and the scope-and-sequence chart show the specific topic and the emphasized skills of each lesson.

> Lesson topics phrased as questions are problems, rather than worksheets. These problems involve numerous skills and focus on historical issues; worksheets focus on a single skill and mix familiar with historical content.

The first four skills (evidence, cause-and-effect, comparison, and generalization) involve both identification and evaluation. A few lessons focus on either identification or evaluation, but most consider both.

The problem lessons ["Salem Witch Trials" (Lesson 10), "The Causes of the Revolution" (Lesson 15), and "Why Was the Constitution Written?" (Lesson 25)], can be used to teach a wide variety of critical thinking skills. The individual teacher will have to decide which skills to emphasize. The skills listed in the scope-and-sequence chart for these lessons are those most obviously targeted.

A look at the historical source books (pp. 129–130 of the student text) shows that the viewpoints in Book 1 are based on major interpretations: Paul Boyer, Stephen Nissenbaum, Chadwick Hausen, and Marion Starkey on the Salem Witch Trials; Bernard Bailyn, Lawrence Gipson, Louis Hacker, and Edmund Morgan on the American Revolution; and Charles Beard, Forrest McDonald, and Clinton Rossiter on the Constitution. In addition, Lesson 23 gives students an opportunity to evaluate a summary of Federalist Paper Number 10 by James Madison against the famous "Brutus" Essay I by the Anti-Federalist Robert Yates. Arguments made by James Madison in three of the Federalist Papers are to be evaluated in Lesson 24.

The Role of the Student

The student book contains "A Guide to Critical Thinking" and twenty-nine historical lessons involving critical thinking. The "Guide to Critical Thinking" is intended to be used when students have a need to learn the components of a particular skill. While some may find it worthwhile to read through the whole Guide to get an overview of the skills involved in argument evaluation, it is not recommended that students study all the various skills at once. Rather, they should refer to the part of the Guide that explains the skill they are currently learning.

The historical lessons consist of both short worksheet problems for practicing skills (1–2 pages each) and longer historical problems (2–25 pages each) with opposing viewpoints. Paragraphs in longer viewpoints are numbered to make discussion and referencing easier.

Particular skills, especially generalizations and cause-and-effect reasoning, are explained with visual models. These have proven helpful for some, and students regularly use them to help evaluate arguments on tests.

These books focus on formulating good arguments as well as evaluating arguments offered by others. In this way, students should begin to question their own assumptions, points of view, and prejudices. This self-criticism, referred to by Richard Paul as "critical thinking in the strong sense," is an important, if difficult, goal to achieve.

This change in student attitudes about the nature of historical knowledge (epistemology) is as important as their mastery of critical thinking skills. As mentioned earlier, students should begin to see historical knowledge as changing, selective, fragmentary, and open to question. Beginning with Worksheet A, students should be encouraged, even expected, to question viewpoints presented. The problem format helps students see history the way it really is and to ask questions. It also makes history much more interesting.

Scope and Sequence of Skills • Book 1

Abbreviations used in this chart are as follows: **(TG)**—Teacher's Guide; **(GTC)**—"Guide to Critical Thinking," Unit 1 in Student Book; **(v)**—Values; **(a)**—eliminating alternatives.

Lesson	Topic	Evidence	Cause/Effect	Comparison	Generalization	Assumption	Relevant Information	Proof
Concrete Example		TG 14	TG 19	TG 39	GCT 8	—	—	—
Explanation		GCT 2	GCT 5	GCT 7	GCT 8	GCT 15	GCT 18	GCT 11

Introductory Worksheets

Lesson	Topic	Evidence	Cause/Effect	Comparison	Generalization	Assumption	Relevant Information	Proof
A	Bermuda Triangle	■	■		■			
B, C, D	Evaluating Evidence	■						
E	Cause and Effect Reasoning		■					
F, G	Evaluating Comparisons			■				
H	Evaluating Generalizations				■			
I, J	Identifying Assumptions					■		

Colonial Period

Lesson	Topic	Evidence	Cause/Effect	Comparison	Generalization	Assumption	Relevant Information	Proof
1	Exploration	■						
2	Early Colonies	■						
3	Early Colonies		■					
4	Early Colonies		■					
5	Exploration	■	■					
6	Early Colonies		■					
7	Roanoke	■						
8	John Smith					■	■	
9	Women in 17th-Century Maryland		■		■	■	■	
10	Salem Witchcraft Trials	■	■		■		■	

Scope and Sequence of Skills • Book 1 (continued)

Revolutionary Period

Lesson	Topic	Evidence	Cause/Effect	Comparison	Generalization	Assumption	Relevant Information	Proof
11	Causes of the Am. Revolution	■						
12	American Revolution			■				
13	American Revolution				■			
14	American Revolution					■		
15	Main Causes of American Revolution	■	■		■	■		
16	Stamp Act	■				■ (v)		
17	Lexington Green	■					■	
18	Pictures as History	■					■	
19	Effects of American Revolution		■			■		

Constitutional Period

Lesson	Topic	Evidence	Cause/Effect	Comparison	Generalization	Assumption	Relevant Information	Proof
20	Weaknesses of Constitutions					■ (v)	■	
21	Shays's Rebellion		■				■	
22	Constitutional Convention	■						
23	Ratification		■	■	■	■		
24	Ratification			■	■	■		
25	Reasons for Constitution	■	■		■			
26	U. S. Constitution: Foreign Views				■	■ (v)		■ (a)
27	Successful Constitutions		■				■	
28	Support for Constitution			■		■		
29	Freedom of Speech			■		■ (v)		

Bibliography of Sources on Critical Thinking

Beyer, Barry. *Practical Strategies for the Teaching of Thinking*. Boston: Allyn and Bacon, 1987.

———— "Teaching Critical Thinking: A Direct Approach." *Social Education* 49 (April 1985): 297–303.

Bloch, Marc. *The Historian's Craft*, New York: Random House, 1953.

Bloom, Benjamin S., ed. *Taxonomy of Educational Objectives, Handbook I: Cognitive Domain*. New York: David McKay, 1956.

Carr, Edward Harlett. *What Is History?* New York: Random House, 1961.

Copi, Irving. *Introduction to Logic*. 5th ed. New York: Macmillan, 1978.

Costa, Arthur. "Teaching For, Of, and About Thinking." In *Developing Minds: A Resource Book for Teaching Thinking*. Edited by Arthur L. Costa, 20–24. Alexandria, VA: Association for Supervision and Curriculum Development, 1985.

———— and Lawrence Lowery. *Techniques for Teaching Thinking*. Pacific Grove, CA: Midwest, 1989.

Crossley, David J., and Peter Wilson. *How to Argue*. New York: Random House, 1979.

Fisher, David Hackett. *Historians' Fallacies: Toward a Logic of Historical Thought*. New York: Harper and Row, 1970.

Gustavson, Carl. *A Preface to History*. New York: McGraw-Hill, 1955.

Norris, Stephen. "The Reliability of Observation Statements." *Rational Thinking Reports*, No. 4. Urbana, IL: University of Illinois, 1979.

———— and Robert Ennis. *Evaluating Critical Thinking*. Pacific Grove, CA: Midwest, 1989.

O'Reilly, Kevin. "Teaching Critical Thinking in High School U.S. History." *Social Education* 49 (April 1985): 281–4.

———— "Vietnam: A Case Study for Critical Thinking" (videotape). Pleasantville, NY: Educational Audiovisual, 1989.

Paul, Richard. "Critical Thinking: Fundamental to Education for a Free Society." *Educational Leadership* 42 (September 1984): 4–14.

Roden, Philip. *The Elusive Truth*. Glenview, IL: Scott-Foresman, 1973.

Sanders, Norris. *Classroom Questions: What Kinds?* New York: Harper and Row, 1966.

Swartz, Robert and D. N. Perkins. *Teaching Thinking: Issues and Approaches*. Pacific Grove, CA: Midwest, 1989.

Weddle, Perry. *Argument: A Guide to Critical Thinking*. New York: McGraw-Hill, 1977.

INTRODUCTORY LESSONS FOR SKILL DEVELOPMENT

Worksheet A: The Bermuda Triangle

Objectives

To increase skepticism of what is read, seen, or heard.
To develop inclination and ability to question statements.

Teaching Ideas

PREPARATION

Give students copies of the first page of the worksheet (page 29) and ask them to write their reaction to it. Do not allow discussion at this point. Check to make sure everyone has written something. If some students say they don't understand what to write, tell them to write down how they feel about the reading, but don't go into any more detail. The whole idea is to avoid giving away what you're looking for in their reactions.

USING THE WORKSHEET

Some students will accept the argument in the handout without any criticisms. Many students feel that anything written down must be true. When the discussion begins they will see that some of their classmates were more skeptical and that the argument shouldn't have been blindly accepted.

When you distribute copies of the Relevant Information sheet, this lesson in skepticism should be reinforced. After students read the relevant information, the author's argument should look very weak.

EXTENDING THE LESSON

This reading might also be used to teach a number of other skills, such as finding the main idea, identifying value and emotional words, identifying assumptions and fallacies, and evaluating evidence.

Suggested Analysis

The author argues that one hundred ships go down each year, but doesn't compare that to the number of ships in the area (ten thousand distress calls) or to the number of sinkings in other areas of the ocean.

In paragraph 6 the author uses the "leading question technique" when he asks why pilot Cosner didn't go on Flight 19. Maybe Cosner was constipated or had the flu. The later suggestion that he had a "peculiar feeling" isn't really argued or supported by evidence. Similarly, the author suggests that the Navy is covering up the situation by not saying anything about it. But maybe the Navy hasn't bothered to deny it because the whole theory is so ridiculous.

Worksheet B: Evaluating Evidence

Objectives

To increase ability in identifying evidence
To increase ability in evaluating evidence

Teaching Ideas
INTRODUCING THE SKILL

To introduce the skills of identifying and evaluating evidence, take five students into the hallway, out of the class's sight, and tell them they are going to role play a murder. Have three students stay near your classroom door, one student go 25 feet down the hall in one direction, and the other student go 25 feet in the opposite direction. Tell them they are to watch carefully. Hand one of the three students by the door a pen and tell him or her to point it at one of the other students in the hall and yell, "Bang!" Tell the "murdered" student to fall down.

Bring the five students back together, and tell them the rest of the class is going to ask them questions to figure out who committed the crime. Only the murderer may lie; the witnesses (everyone else in the hall) must tell the truth. Tell the other witnesses they must tell everything they know. They are not to hide information or try to confuse the class.

When using this in class, substitute the corresponding student name for each of the roles in italics.

Re-enter the classroom with the five students. Tell the class that *the victim* was just killed, and have that person sit down. Tell the class that their task is to figure out who did it by questioning the four witnesses. [At some point a student may ask where the murder weapon is. If so, produce the pen (tell them it's a poison-dart gun) and ask if they have any questions about the weapon. If they ask about fingerprints, say that only *the murderer's* fingerprints are on it.] Later, tell the class that you have a letter, dated a month ago, written by *the murderer* to a close friend saying he or she was going to get even with *the victim*. Don't be discouraged if the students don't ask very good questions. Even advanced classes have had difficulty with this introductory exercise.

After ten–fifteen minutes, tell the class that you're going to stop talking about who committed the murder and, instead, talk about the skill involved in trying to decide who did it. This is the metacognitive stage. Ask the class what they think evidence is. [Based on this activity: statements by witnesses, objects that were part of the event, or written documents.]

The best way to get at the criteria for evaluating evidence is to ask the general question: How did you decide which evidence to believe? This way the class will generate the criteria themselves. If the general question proves too difficult you can ask more specific questions:

Ask the class why they didn't believe *the murderer* when he said he didn't do it. [He had a reason to lie to protect himself.] Suppose *the murderer* said *a witness* did it, and *that witness* said *the murderer* did it, and that's all the class knew. Could they have told who was guilty? [No.] So why did they believe *that witness* over *the murderer* now? [Because other witnesses supported *that witness's* version by saying *the murderer* did it.] Suppose a third witness was around the corner when the murder occurred. Would that strengthen or weaken his/her evidence? [Weaken it.] Why? [The testimony is now given by someone who did not see the crime—a secondary source.] Is *the murderer* more likely to tell the truth in the trial or in a letter to a friend? [This is tricky, but the private letter is generally more reliable.]

REVIEWING THE SKILL

Write the criteria for evaluating evidence (see section on **Evaluation** in the "Guide to Critical Thinking," student text, page 5) on the board and have students copy it into their notebooks. You could also ask a volunteer to make a poster to remind students of the criteria (below).

EVALUATING EVIDENCE

Is there a source for the information?

If no, the information is unsupported and weakened.

If yes, evaluate it:

      P — primary or secondary?

      R — reason to lie or exaggerate?

      O — other evidence to verify this evidence?

      P — public or private?

This process of making posters for the classroom can be repeated for other skills and their criteria.

USING THE WORKSHEET

When the class has completed the role-play activity and the discussion, you can pass out Worksheet B (pp. 31–32) as an immediate follow-up on evaluating evidence. Tell the students they are going to practice what they have just learned about evaluating evidence.

Suggested Answers

- The jury was probably right in its guilty verdict.

Point out that making the historical judgment that Lucky stabbed John Jones is not the same as finding him guilty in court. In history, unlike in court, we do not have to prove something "beyond a reasonable doubt," but rather provide enough evidence to show that the person probably did it. In other words, we might say we think Lucky committed the murder, but should have been found "not guilty" in court. We do not presume innocence in history as we do in trials.

A. Statements are numbers 1–10, 12, 15–17.

B. Documents are numbers 14 and 18.

C. Objects are numbers 11 and 13.

- The evidence is evaluated as follows.

Factor	4	7	10	11	14	17	18
P	no	yes	yes	yes	yes	no	no
R	no	no	yes	yes	yes	yes	yes
O	no	yes	yes	yes	yes	yes	yes
P	no	no	no	yes	yes	yes	yes

- Since evidence 18 is private and seems to have no reason to lie, it is more reliable than evidence 4. Not foolproof; just more likely to be reliable.

Worksheet C: Sources and Evidence

Objectives

To identify sources
To evaluate evidence

Teaching Ideas
Using the Worksheet

Students must first determine if a source for the information is given. Then, if there is a source, they are to evaluate it according to the four questions explained in the handout.

Distribute copies of the worksheet and ask the students to complete as much as they can. Remind them that a longer explanation of evidence can be found on pages 2–4 in Unit 1 of their book.

When students have filled in as much of the sheet as they can, have them compare answers in groups of three. Finally, discuss the worksheet as a class.

Suggested Answers

1. Since the statement gives no source for the information, it cannot be further evaluated. Thus, the evidence is not well supported.

    [You will need to point out to some students that even though a specific figure ($15 million) is used, we don't know where the figure came from; no source is given.]

2. The scorebook is the source for the statistic. **P**—It is a primary source, since the scorekeeper had to be at the games; **R**—there is no reason for the scorebook (or scorekeeper) to lie about hits and times at bat (batting average); **O**—there is no other evidence given to support the claim that Kurt is a great hitter; **P**—it is a public statement. **Overall**, this would be considered a reliable source.

3. The three workers' statements at the public hearings are the source. **P**—The workers say they saw payoffs, so they are primary sources; **R**—the workers might have motives to lie or exaggerate if they don't like Mayor Salza; **O**—the three workers verify each other; **P**—these are public statements. **Overall**, the fact that three people were willing to risk testifying about the corruption does carry some weight, although the evidence isn't as reliable as that in problem 2.

4. There is no source given for the information, so it is not well supported.

Worksheet D: Evaluating Evidence

Objective

To evaluate sources of evidence

Teaching Ideas
USING THE WORKSHEET

Pass out the worksheet. Ask the students to fill it in then discuss their answers as a class. If students are confused about any of the criteria, the following questions may help them clarify their evaluations.

QUESTIONS FOR DETERMINING EVIDENCE

- To determine if someone is a **primary source**, ask, "Was this person at the location when the event occurred, or was she talking about herself?"

- To determine if someone has a **reason to lie**, ask, "Did this person make him- or herself look good by the statement?" [Why would he lie to make himself look bad?]

- To determine if there is **other supporting evidence**, ask, "Who said this? Did any other people say the same thing?"

- To determine if the evidence is **public**, ask, "Did this person make the statement to influence anyone else? Does he or she think anyone other than the person spoken to would hear what was said?"

Suggested Answers

1. Yu-chi **P**—is a primary source, **R**—has a reason to lie, and **O**—presents no supporting evidence. **P**—the statement is public, meant to influence his father. **Overall**, the evidence isn't very reliable because of the reason to lie and the lack of supporting evidence.

2. Laura **P**—is a primary source about talking with Jill (but she wasn't at the scene of the babysitting), **R**—may have a reason to lie if she wants to protect Jill (we don't know), **O**—has supporting evidence provided by Connie's and Ellen's statements. **P**—the statement is public, meant to influence Bob. **Overall**, this is fairly good evidence.

3. Christie **P**—is a primary source, **R**—has no reason to lie, as her statement places the blame on herself, **O**—offers no supporting evidence. **P**—it is a public statement. **Overall**, Christie's evidence is strong. [Admitting you've done wrong is unlikely to be a lie, but it is possible—for example, if she had failed because she had skipped school, which might have gotten her into worse trouble.]

Worksheet E: Cause and Effect

Objectives

To recognize cause-and-effect reasoning
To evaluate cause-and-effect reasoning

Teaching Ideas
INTRODUCING THE SKILL

Introduce cause-and-effect reasoning by telling the class that you, the teacher, just entered the emergency room with a terrible pain in your stomach. They are the doctors on duty. What would they ask? Set it up that you have been at the beach all day and left your ham and mayonnaise sandwich out in the hot sun.

Although some student may focus on what you ate and the likelihood of food poisoning early in the discussion, other students may later ask questions about appendicitis, medication, and alcohol. They are considering other possible causes for the problem. You could ask the class how they could test their hypothesis further to focus them on the connection between each proposed cause and effect. How could they check to be more certain it was food poisoning from the ham or mayonnaise? (A blood test showing bacteria in the blood would show a connection).

REINFORCING THE SKILL

While these questions for evaluating cause-and-effect reasoning are being discussed, write them on the chalkboard. As with evaluating evidence, the students should be instructed to copy the questions into their notebooks and someone should make a poster to be put up in the classroom. For further discussion of this skill, refer students to the **Cause-and-Effect Reasoning** section of the "Guide to Critical Thinking" (pp. 5–7 in their text).

USING THE WORKSHEET

Once you have laid out the steps in evaluating cause and effect reasoning you can pass out Worksheet E for students to try for guided practice. When they have completed the worksheet, have them compare answers in small groups or in a whole-class discussion.

Suggested Answers

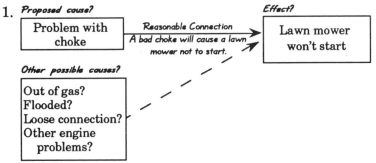

1.

Overall, this is not very strong reasoning, since other possible causes have not been ruled out.

Overall, this is very strong reasoning, since other possible causes have been ruled out.

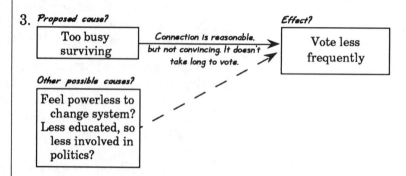

Overall, the other possible causes seem as important to the effect as the proposed cause. It is not a very strong argument.

Worksheet F: Comparison Arguments

Objective

To introduce criteria for evaluating comparisons

Teaching Ideas

INTRODUCING THE SKILL

Have students do the introductory problem first. Make sure they write down their questions, then discuss the problem as a class.

After they have given their answers to the autocross problem, ask students what questions they ask to evaluate comparisons in general? (How are the two cases different?) If necessary, refer students to the section on **Comparisons** in the "Guide to Critical Thinking" (pp. 7–8 in the student text).

USING THE WORKSHEET

When students are ready to evaluate the comparison arguments, have them write their answers individually, then discuss the problems in small groups. Note to students that in Problem 3, since Candice is arguing that the radios are different, the students should focus on identifying similarities.

Suggested Answers

INTRODUCTORY PROBLEM

Some Autocross Race questions to ask:

1. What kind of car were you driving?
2. Was it the same course?
3. What were the weather conditions?

Emphasize to the students that they already know how to evaluate comparison arguments. They just showed it by the questions they asked.

COMPARISONS

1. Margarine substitute

   — Compared: butter and margarine

   — Possible differences: taste; amount or type of fat

   — Possible similarities: function in baking

   — Overall: They are similar enough to allow the cake to still come out as a cake, although there might be some difference in taste and texture. To demonstrate the similarities between butter and margarine, ask students what would happen if they substituted jelly for butter.

2. Statewide test

   — Compared: Student performance on one test at Centralville and Evantown

[2.] — Possible differences:

a. The student body of the two schools might be very different. For example, students might vary in educational background, ethnic background, economic opportunities, or social class.

b. The test may have been given in different grades in the two schools.

c. The curriculum at Centralville might be more suited to the test.

d. Testing circumstances at the two schools may have differed; e.g., physical testing environment; attitudes of students toward test; school activities before or after test, etc.

—Possible similarities: All above items might be similar rather than different.

—Overall: Not enough information is given. If most or all of the above items are different, then the comparison is very weak.

3. Deluxe Radio

—Compared: deluxe and standard radio models

—Possible differences: Cost is the only known difference; number of stations and sound quality are implied differences.

—Possible similarities: We don't know if the standard radio can also do the things the deluxe model can do.

—Overall: Candice has not drawn a reasonable conclusion. She may be satisfied with the radio, but she has not shown that the extra $50 was worth it. If the standard radio plays all the stations she likes and has a clear sound, then Candice's money was not well spent. In this comparison, the possible similarities undermine the argument because Candice is arguing they are different and that the difference makes the extra money spent worthwile.

Worksheet G: Understanding Comparisons

Objectives

To identify comparison reasoning
To evaluate comparison arguments

Teaching Ideas

Have students write their answers individually, then discuss and defend their answers in small groups. Or you can discuss answers as a class.

Suggested Answers

• Numbers **1** and **5** are comparisons. Other items may have comparisons implied in them, but the comparison is not a key part of the argument.

8.	A	11.	D	14.	D
9.	D	12.	A		
10.	D	13.	A		

15. a. Compares John's taste in movies to mine.

    b. It's an alike comparison.

    c. Since John is different from me in some ways, his taste in movies is likely to be different from mine in some ways.

    d. If John's movie taste is different from mine in a way that's important for this movie, then it might be a poor comparison. For example, if John doesn't mind violence in movies but I do, and if this movie is violent, then the comparison argument is faulty.

16. a. Compares Wranglers' team record to Panthers' team record.

    b. It's a different comparison (claims that since they are different from each other in a particular way they are different in other particular ways also).

    c. Additional information would be needed in the areas of number of games and opponents. They may be similar or different.

    d. The more similarities that are found between the two teams, the stronger the argument that the Wranglers' team is better.

17. a. Compares state university to private college.

    b. It's an alike comparison.

c. Areas of possible comparison might include social life, facilities, library sources, cost, etc.

d. Maybe other aspects of the private college are better. On the other hand, if the campus and professors are the most important considerations to Carrie, then this is a good comparison.

18. a. Compares the private college to public colleges. (The comparison is implicit in "extra money.")

b. It is a difference comparison.

c–d. Since the statement doesn't say that the soccer team and the professors are better than at other, less expensive schools, there is no basis for making the claim that the extra money was worth it.

Worksheet H: Evaluating Generalizations

Objective

To recognize and evaluate generalizations

Teaching Ideas

USING THE WORKSHEET

The first worksheet section focuses on evaluating generalization claims. A circle diagram is shown for the example problem. If students find such diagrams helpful, encourage them to draw their own for problems 1–3.

The second section of the worksheet focuses on how far given information may be generalized. There is room for reasonable disagreement on these questions, so try to avoid pushing for one right answer. Ask students for the reasons for their answers. Focus on the subgroups of the major group in the generalization.

You might want to have the class read over the section on generalizations in the "Guide to Critical Thinking." If not, you can refer them to that section if they need help.

Suggested Answers

1. a. The generalization is that most kids in the school watch more than 12 hours of television a week.

   b. Subgroups might include honors, average, or remedial students; those involved in extracurricular activities and those who aren't; students who have jobs and those who don't; students from various income levels; students of various home environments, and so forth.

   c. The sample is relatively small (30 out of 800, or about 4%).

   d. The sample may have most of the subgroups by random distribution, but since it is a specific class, it is an ability group.

   e. This isn't a great sample because the amount of homework generally affects how much television a student watches. If this is a remedial class, the number of hours watched probably is not the same as the number of hours watched by honors students.

2. a. The generalization is that all Italians belong to the Mafia.

   b. Subgroups include different intelligence levels, different levels of education, income, and occupation; different geographic locations; different family lives and background; and so forth.

c. The sample may be exceedingly small (this person may know one Italian who belongs to the Mafia), somewhat larger (the person may live in an Italian neighborhood and know many Italians), or nonexistent (the person may have heard that Italians belong to the Mafia). Even with the larger sample, however, it is very small compared to the millions of Italians in the world.

d. We don't know much about the sample, but we can say with reasonable assurance that not all the subgroups are represented well.

e. This is a poor generalization. It is a good example of a stereotype—a large, complex group of people being simplified to all having a particular characteristic.

3. a. The generalization is that the population of Mudville rose dramatically in the 1970s.

b. As far as we know, the sample covers everyone in the large group (Mudville).

c. The generalization is very strong, which tells us that census records are good sources.

4. Neither A nor D are reasonable extensions of the information in your sample, since both contain nonpublic, nonsuburban, and nonsecondary schools. (Is homework a key to good grades in elementary schools?) B, although restricted to your own suburban district, is weak for one of the same reasons that A and D are weak: it includes elementary schools. C is the best of the given choices. It is restricted to public suburban high schools, although it does extend the sample generalization too far geographically.

5. D is the best choice, since it is the only one that emphasizes both the mountains and a strong defense. A emphasizes only defense, and it is unclear how being large or small affects avoiding war (B and C).

6. A is the best choice. The students in your school may be different (for example, in terms of educational or cultural background) from those in other schools, which makes it difficult to extend the sample beyond your own school (B and C). The information you have says nothing about the type of music students do not like.

Worksheet I: Identifying Assumptions—1

Objectives

To recognize arguments based on assumptions
To identify assumptions made by others

Teaching Ideas
INTRODUCING THE SKILL

To encourage students to begin recognizing their own assumptions, give half the class statement 1 and the other half statement 2 (below). Ask them to write an answer to the question. Don't say they have different statements.

1. "The Soviet Union gives a great deal of economic aid to India." Why do you think the Soviet Union does this?

2. "The United States gives a great deal of economic aid to India." Why do you think the United States does this?

When each student has written a response, list the various reasons on the chalkboard and ask the students to count the number of positive and negative motives attributed to each country. Were more positive motives given to the United States? If so, why?

Students may contend that the Soviet Union is an expansionist country which is trying to spread communism. The question "How do you know they are expansionist?" will force them to examine how they arrived at their belief. Similarly, "How do you know the United States is giving aid for humanitarian reasons?" will force them to question how they arrived at that belief. While it *may* be true that Soviet aid is self-serving and American aid is humanitarian, students should examine how they arrived at these beliefs. Did they have supporting evidence or did their frame of reference lead to the assumption?

USING THE WORKSHEET

It is probably better to start with this worksheet rather than Worksheet J. If students can identify the assumptions on this worksheet, then they probably don't need the more structured approach.

Suggested Answers

1. Your brother gets good grades in school because he studies. Your lower grades in school are due to lack of study (as opposed to other reasons).

2. Peter is the same age as (or older than) Marie.

3. You run faster than I do.

4. You don't have good writing skills.

5. I don't have other unexpected expenses. I'll be alive. I'll be able to drive.

6. Drinking is a way to enjoy life. Jim is too serious.

Worksheet J: Identifying Assumptions—2

Objective

To provide a structured approach to identifying assumptions in arguments

Teaching Ideas

It is probably a good idea to start assumptions with Introductory Worksheet I. If students can identify the assumptions in that worksheet, then they may not need this more structured approach. You may also choose to use this step-by-step approach with only a few students.

If you do use this worksheet, have the students discuss problem 1 as a class before they go on. Give students time to do problem 2 individually, then discuss their answers. Repeat this procedure for problem 3.

Suggested Answers

2. Step 1: (Premise) "Because" Fred works for a station which does fine work...

    Step 2: (Conclusion) "Therefore," Fred is a good mechanic.

    Step 3: (Unique parts) works for a station which does fine work/good mechanic

    Step 4: (Assumption) "People" who work for a station which does fine mechanical work must be good mechanics.

3. Step 1: (Premise) "Because" Sequoia is in the band (and Leona isn't)...

    Step 2: (Conclusion) "Therefore," Sequoia is a better musician (than Leona).

    Step 3: (Unique parts) in the band/better musician

    Step 4: (Assumption) "People" who are in a band are better musicians (than those who aren't).

WORKSHEET A   The Bermuda Triangle

(1) The Bermuda Triangle—an area roughly from Bermuda, southwest to Florida, then east out into the Atlantic, and then northwest back to Bermuda—is one of the most dangerous and strange spots on earth. Beginning back in the 1600s and continuing to today, the number of ships lost in the Triangle is staggering. In recent years an average of about one hundred ships and many airplanes have been lost in the area each year. It is common knowledge among commercial pilots and ship captains that the Triangle is a dangerous place.

(2) What has happened to these boats and planes is especially mysterious, however, and that is what gives the area its name as the "Devil's Triangle." For example, a boat named the *Hollyhock* was off the coast of Florida when it suddenly lost radio contact with the coast. Later, it picked up California on the radio. Then it spotted land on its monitors where there was no land! The *Hollyhock* disappeared without a trace.

(3) Another boat, the *Witchcraft*, was at Buoy Number 7, only two miles off the coast of Miami, when the owner radioed to the Coast Guard for assistance because the boat was taking on water. He reassured the Coast Guard, however, that the boat was in no serious danger, for it had built-in flotation chambers. When the Coast Guard arrived at Buoy Number 7, the *Witchcraft* had vanished.

(4) Airplanes, too, have had bizarre incidents. The *Star Tiger*, flying over the Devil's Triangle, suddenly lost all radio contact. No wreckage of the plane was ever found. In 1963 two KC-135 jet tankers disappeared three hundred miles southwest of Bermuda. What caused these planes to go down?

(5) Probably the most incredible incident concerned Training Flight 19, which took off from Fort Lauderdale, Florida, on December 5, 1945. Five Avenger aircraft took off that day on a regular Navy training flight. Pilot Cosner did not go on the flight. Why not? Commander Taylor also seemed hesitant. Did he have the same peculiar feeling as Cosner? The flight was routine at first, but then mysterious things started to happen. The pilots seemed confused and their instruments were doing weird things. The air base which had radio contact with the planes heard the pilots say, "Which way is west?" and the phrases "upside down" and "white water." The planes kept changing directions, almost flying in circles. Then—silence. A search plane was sent out and it, too, disappeared. The Navy has kept the incident quiet, and it hasn't denied the stories that authors have written about it.

(6) It is difficult to explain what happens in the Devil's Triangle. Some people believe there is a magnetic field which throws everything off. Others believe it has to do with the lost continent of Atlantis. Whatever the cause, it is worth thinking about twice before traveling through this area—one of the strangest spots on our earth.

Relevant Information on the Bermuda Triangle

1. The *Star Tiger*'s flight was at night in poor weather.

2. It is not unheard of, although it is infrequent, for boats out in the ocean to pick up distant areas on the radio.

3. Rain clouds can sometimes look like land on radar.

4. The *Witchcraft* was out in bad weather.

5. Coast Guard reports make no mention of the *Witchcraft* being near Buoy Number 7. An author estimated the location by comparing several reports.

6. It would have taken the Coast Guard about twenty minutes to get from their station to where the *Witchcraft* was.

7. In twenty minutes a boat in calm seas can drift about one mile.

8. It is extremely difficult to find the wreckage of a plane or boat in the ocean, even on a clear day.

9. Debris found in one spot in the ocean contained the serial numbers of both KC-135 jet tankers. Some observers say this indicates that the two planes collided in the air.

10. The editor of *Aviation Week* stated that, based on a statistical analysis of the number of accidents in an area compared with the number of flights in that area, the Bermuda Triangle is one of the safest spots in the world. It is a popular area with pilots.

11. An Avenger aircraft will sink into the ocean roughly forty-five seconds after splashing down.

12. Two of the men who were in the radio tower in Fort Lauderdale at the time of Training Flight 19 do not recall the Avenger pilots saying "Which way is west?" or "upside down" or "white water." These two men say the planes were definitely lost.

13. Commander Taylor of Training Flight 19 radioed, "If we fly north, then east, we'll get home." He also mentioned being over the Keys (islands). He may have thought he was over the Florida Keys, when actually he was over the Grand Keys in the Atlantic. His proposed course of "north, then east" would have taken the planes toward the middle of the Atlantic.

14. At the time that radio contact with the plane sent to search for Training Flight 19 was lost, people on the coast saw what looked like an explosion near the search plane's last-reported location.

15. Out of 10,000 distress calls made to the Coast Guard, about 100 ships are lost in the Bermuda Triangle each year.

16. According to the Coast Guard, many pleasure boat owners don't know what they're doing in the ocean. For example, when the Coast Guard told one owner to plot a course toward an island, the owner said he couldn't find it on his map. The Coast Guard asked him what map he was using, and he said he was looking at the world atlas.

17. Each author who writes about the Bermuda Triangle describes a triangle of a different size and shape from the other authors.

18. The author of this Bermuda Triangle article writes books on popular subjects, such as mysterious and bizarre phenomena.

WORKSHEET B   Evaluating Evidence

Background

You, as a historian, are trying to decide who stabbed John Jones in 1940 in the corridor at your school. You have gathered the following information (evidence) about the case.

Relevant Information

A. The report on the police investigation into the death of John Jones says:
1. The police concluded that he was murdered by stab wounds.
2. The police had three suspects: 1) Kid Kelly, 2) Slim Stowell, and 3) Lucky Levin. All three were in the corridor within ten feet of Jones when he was murdered.
3. Police thought they had enough evidence to prosecute Lucky Levin.

B. Lucky Levin was tried for the alleged murder of John Jones. In the trial:
4. Lucky's girlfriend said he was a good person and would never kill anyone.
5. A teacher testified he opened the door of his room and entered the corridor as soon as he heard John Jones scream. No one could have moved, and no one was moving when he looked into the corridor. Jones was lying on the floor while Lucky, Kid, and Slim were standing within ten feet, looking at him. Lucky was closest to Jones.
6. Kid testified that he didn't do it, but he was looking the other way so he doesn't know whether Lucky or Slim did it.
7. Slim testified that he didn't do it, Lucky did it.
8. Lucky testified that he didn't do it, Slim did it.
9. Witness A, who didn't know any of the men, said he heard Jones say, "No, Lucky, no" right before the murder.
10. Witness B, who was 35 feet away and who didn't know any of the men, said he saw Lucky stab Jones.
11. The knife was shown to have Lucky's, and only Lucky's, fingerprints on it.
12. According to Kid, both Lucky and Slim had knives with them on the day of the death.
13. The police found a knife on Slim at the scene of the murder, as well as the knife in Jones. No other weapons were found.
14. An IOU note produced at the trial showed that Jones owed Lucky $300, which had been due to be paid three days before the murder.
15. Witness C testified that Slim did not like Jones.
16. Witness D, 50 feet away, testified that she saw Lucky stab Jones.
17. Witness E, in another part of the building and not within sight of the murder scene, says he's sure Lucky killed Jones.
18. At the trial, a letter from Lucky's girlfriend to her mother was introduced as evidence. The letter said that Lucky hated John Jones.

C. The jury found Lucky guilty of murder.

Evaluate the Evidence

Q As a historian, do you think the jury was right in its verdict? Why do you think so?

Q Give one example from the Relevant Information section on page 31 for each type of evidence listed below. Write the number of the evidence on the line provided.

_____ A. Statements by witnesses

_____ B. Documents (written information)

_____ C. Objects

Q Evaluate (judge) the following evidence selected from the Relevant Information. Use the **PROP** factors (criteria) from the section on **Evidence** in the "Guide to Critical Thinking."

Factor #	4	7	10	11	14	17	18
P							
R							
O							
P							

Q Compare the reliability of evidence 4 and evidence 18. Which is more reliable? Explain your answer.

WORKSHEET C   Sources and Evidence

Whenever you see information used in support of an argument you should ask certain questions, the first and most important being, "Does the information have a source given?"

A *source* is the person, place, or written document the information came from. If there is no given source, the information cannot be evaluated and should not be accepted as reliable.

If the information does give a source, you can evaluate its reliability by asking a number of questions, four of which are given here. For further help, see the section on **Evidence** in the "Guide to Critical Thinking."

Criteria for Evaluating Evidence

P   Is it a **primary** (more reliable) or secondary (less reliable) source?

R   Does the person giving the evidence have no **reason to lie** (more reliable)?

O   Is there **other evidence** which supports or verifies what this evidence says (more reliable) or is this the only evidence presented on the topic (less reliable)?

P   Is it a public (less reliable) or **private** (more reliable) statement? It is public if the person giving it knew other people would read or see it.

 Evaluate each of the following arguments using the above questions.

1.   The city government under Mayor Elwell was very corrupt. Over $15 million was stolen in only five years.

   Is there a source given for any information in this argument? _____
   If not, the claim of corruption is not well supported by evidence.
   If yes, evaluate the evidence and explain your evaluation.

   P

   R

   O

   P

---

2.   Kurt is a great hitter. The statistics from last season's scorebook show he
      hit .457, a very high average.

      Is there a source given for any information in this argument? _____

      If not, the argument is not well supported. If yes, evaluate it.

        P

        R

        O

        P

3.   The city government under Mayor Salza was very corrupt. Three city
      workers stated in public hearings that they each had seen money paid to
      city officials for special favors.

      Is there a source given for any information in this argument? _____

      If not, the argument is not well supported. If yes, evaluate it.

        P

        R

        O

        P

4.   Kelley is a great hitter. She can hit the fastball and the curve.

      Is there a source given for any information in this argument? _____

      If not, the argument is not well supported. If yes, evaluate it.

        P

        R

        O

        P

WORKSHEET D   Evaluating Evidence

You will recall that the first question you should ask about information (evidence) is whether or not a source is given. Each argument on this worksheet names the source, or the person who said it. For further explanation see the section on **Evidence** in the "Guide to Critical Thinking."

Criteria for Evaluating Evidence

P   Is it a **primary** (more reliable) or secondary (less reliable) source?

R   Does the person giving the evidence have no **reason to lie** (more reliable)?

O   Is there **other evidence** which supports or verifies what this evidence says (more reliable) or is this the only evidence presented on the topic (less reliable)?

P   Is it a public (less reliable) or **private** (more reliable) statement? It is public if the person giving it knew other people would read or see it.

Q Evaluate each of the following situations according to the four criteria given below.

1. Yu-chi tells his father it was not his fault that he got detention. He said that the teacher thought he was talking during class, but he wasn't.

    Evaluate Yu-chi's evidence according to the four criteria.

    P

    R

    O

    P

    Overall, how reliable is Yu-chi's evidence?

---

2. Bob is angry because he thinks his girlfriend, Jill, went out with Larry on Friday. Laura, Connie, and Ellen all told Bob that they had talked with Jill on the phone most of the night on Friday while she was babysitting, so she couldn't have gone out with Larry.

   Evaluate Laura's evidence according to the four criteria.

   P

   R

   O

   P

   Overall, how reliable is Laura's evidence?

3. Christie tells her parents she failed English because she didn't study. She says she has no one to blame but herself and has to admit she deserves to be grounded.

   Evaluate Christie's evidence about why she failed.

   P

   R

   O

   P

   Overall, how reliable is Christie's evidence?

WORKSHEET E   Evaluating Cause-and-Effect Reasoning

When someone proposes a cause for some situation or event, he or she is using cause-and-effect reasoning. Following these steps will help you evaluate such arguments.

EVALUATING CAUSE-AND-EFFECT REASONING

1. Decide which is the cause and which is the effect.

2. See if the person explains how the cause led to the effect. If the person doesn't explain, we should ask if there is a reasonable connection between the cause and the effect.

3. Ask if there are other possible causes for this effect. Has this person eliminated these other possible causes?

Q Using a diagram like the one shown after the first problem will help you follow these steps when evaluating cause-and-effect reasoning. Draw your own diagrams for the other problems.

1. The repairman says that Mark's lawn mower won't start because of a problem with the choke, which will cost $25.00 to fix.

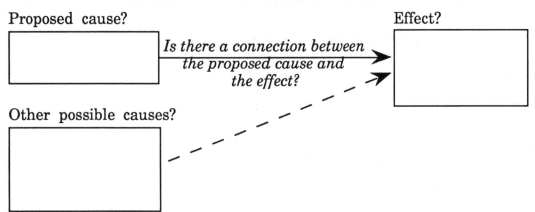

Proposed cause?

Is there a connection between the proposed cause and the effect?

Effect?

Other possible causes?

Overall, how strong is the repairman's cause-and-effect reasoning?

2. Mr. Alberti insulated his house before this winter started. The average temperature this winter has been about the same as last winter, and Mr. Alberti has kept the thermostat at the same settings both winters. So far, he has used 40% fewer gallons of oil than he had at this time last winter. He thinks the insulation has been very effective in saving heating oil.

   Analyze Mr. Alberti's cause-and-effect thinking. Use a diagram.

   Overall, how strong is the argument?

3. Low-income people tend to vote less frequently than high-income people because poorer people are so busy trying to survive that they don't take time to vote.

   Draw a diagram and analyze this thinking.

   Overall, how strong is the argument?

WORKSHEET F   Comparison Arguments

Introductory Problem

Suppose you drove in an autocross race at the North Shore Shopping Center parking lot a month ago. ("Autocross" is a race over a winding course set up with cone markers. Cars race one at a time and are clocked as they run the course.) You drove your 1952 Plymouth, and your time was 36.8 seconds. Now, suppose Harry told you that last Sunday he was in an autocross and his time was 28.2 seconds. He says this proves he is a better driver than you are.

Write three questions that you would want to ask Harry.

1.

2.

3.

Evaluating Comparison Arguments

A comparison argument reasons that since two cases are similar in some respects they will also be similar in another way. You can tell from the questions you wrote above that the key to deciding the strength of a comparison argument is asking, "How are the two cases different?" Refer the the section on **Comparison Reasoning** in the "Guide to Critical Thinking" (Unit 1) if you need more help.

 Using the given questions, evaluate each of the following comparison arguments.

1.   You are baking a cake and the recipe calls for 5 teaspoons of butter. You have no butter, so you reason that if you substitute 5 teaspoons of margarine the cake will still turn out fine.

   a.   What two items are being compared?

   b.   How are they different?

   c.   How are they alike?

   d.   Overall, how strong is this comparison argument?

2.   "The average score on the state-wide test was 12 points higher at Centralville High than it was at Evantown High. It is clear from these scores that the teachers at Centralville are doing a better job of teaching."

    a.   What two items are being compared?

    b.   How are they different?

    c.   How are they alike?

    d.   Overall, how strong is this comparison argument?

3.   Candice paid $50 more to get the deluxe model when she bought her radio. She thinks the money was well spent because the radio gets all the stations she likes and the sound is very clear.

    a.   What two items are being compared?

    b.   How are they different?

    c.   How are they alike?

    d.   Overall, how strong is this comparison argument?

WORKSHEET G   Understanding Comparisons

For help, refer to the section about **Comparisons** in the "Guide to Critical Thinking."

Identifying Comparisons

Q Put a "C" on the line in front of each of the following arguments or claims that use comparison reasoning.

_____ 1. Jean felt the suede jacket was worth the extra money.

_____ 2. Benji has been a great dog. He's very obedient and he doesn't bark much.

_____ 3. Fred used his new equipment the last time he climbed.

_____ 4. I decided to read *A Tale of Two Cities* because, although it is long, it is an excellent story.

_____ 5. You should buy alkaline batteries; they last longer than regular ones.

_____ 6. Tom and Pat helped us out a lot when we had to fix the house. They are good neighbors.

_____ 7. Tomika hit the other car when she backed up in the parking lot.

Categorizing Comparisons

Q Mark each of the following arguments. Put an **S** in front of arguments which claim that the two cases are basically similar. Put a **D** in front of arguments which claim that the two cases are basically different. Remember, better/worse comparisons emphasize differences.

_____ 8. You gave Mari $5.00 for her work, so you should give me $5.00 for my work, too.

_____ 9. Since our team has won more games this year than last, we must have improved.

_____ 10. Rachel is the right player to guard their scorer. Julie just isn't as good on defense.

_____ 11. The new deluxe sedan costs a little more but it's well worth it. It has cruise control and an engine.

_____ 12. I beat George at chess last time, so I'm sure I will again.

_____ 13. Jim has never charged us more than $50.00 for a repair in the past, so he surely won't charge us too much this time.

_____ 14. I'm sticking with Toni because she's a better computer programmer than Geoffrey is.

Analyzing and Evaluating Comparisons

 Each of the following problems presents a comparison argument for you to analyze and evaluate. The **Example** is done for you.

Example:

"I jumped 5'6" in the last meet, so I should jump at least 5'6" today.

    a.   What are the two cases or characteristics being compared?

        Case A: [The speaker's jumping ability at the last meet]

        Case B: [The speaker's jumping ability today]

    b.   Is this an alike or different comparison?

        [Alike]

    c.   What similarities or differences are there between the two cases?

        [Similarities: same goal in same event]

        [Differences: the jumper's health or condition may be different today; weather, jumping conditions, or training time may differ]

    d.   How strong is the comparison?

        [It's reasonable, but it should take into account the possible differences. For example, if the jumper claimed to be in better condition now and the weather is favorable, then the conclusion would be stronger.]

15.   "My best friend, John, liked the movie, so I bet I'll like it too."

    a.   What are the two cases or characteristics being compared? Be precise!

        Case A:

        Case B:

    b.   Is this an alike or different comparison?

    c.   What similarities or differences are there between the two cases?

    d.   How strong is the comparison?

16.   "The Wranglers have a better team than the Panthers. The Wranglers have more wins and fewer losses."

    a.   What are the two cases or characteristics being compared?

        Case A:

        Case B:

    b.   Is this an alike or different comparison?

c. What similarities or differences are there between the two cases?

d. How strong is the comparison?

17. Carrie decided that the state university is just as good as the private college in her area. The campus and the professors at the state university are as good as those at the private college.
    a. What are the two cases or characteristics being compared?
       Case A:

       Case B:

    b. Is this an alike or different comparison?

    c. What similarities or differences are there between the two cases?

    d. How strong is the comparison?

18. Roger decides that the extra money he spends to attend the private college is well worth it. The soccer team is excellent at the private college, as are the professors.
    a. What are the two cases or characteristics being compared?
       Case A:

       Case B:

    b. Is this an alike or different comparison?

    c. What similarities or differences are there between the two cases?

    d. How strong is the comparison?

WORKSHEET H   Evaluating Generalizations (Samples)

If you need help, refer to the definition and examples of **Generalization** in the "Guide to Critical Thinking." Remember that a circle diagram is useful to help visualize generalizations as an analysis aid. An example is done for you.

Example:

"Most American adults would like to own their own homes. Just last month a survey of 1232 students at five hundred colleges around the country showed that 62% of those students who responded want to own their own home."

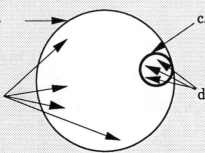

a. What generalization is being made about the whole group?

c. How large is the sample?

b. What subgroups make up the whole group?

d. Does the sample have all the same subgroups in the same proportion as the whole group?

a. Generalization?
   [Most American adults want to own homes.]

b. Subgroups of whole group?
   [Subgroups include men and women and various geographic regions, ages, incomes, and levels of education.]

c. Size of sample?
   [The sample is rather small, compared to the number of people in the whole group, so representativeness will be important.]

d. Representativeness of sample?
   [The sample includes men and women (probably) from different geographic regions, but is not representative in any other way. The sample consists of people who are young, have a relatively high level of income, and have a uniformly high level of education.]

e. Overall, how strong is the generalization?
   [This is a very weak sample; therefore, it is not a good generalization.]

Q Evaluate the following generalizations. Draw a circle graph and use the given questions to help with your evaluation.

1. "Most students in this high school [800 students] watch more than twelve hours of television a week. We took a poll in my social studies class, and twenty out of the thirty students said they watch more than twelve hours a week." [This school has honors, average, and remedial classes.]

[1.] a. Generalization?

   b. Subgroups of whole group?

   c. Size of sample?

   d. Representativeness of sample?

   e. Strength of generalization?

2. "I wouldn't hire an Italian if I were you. They all belong to the Mafia. Pretty soon you'll start having problems."
   a. Generalization?

   b. Subgroups of whole group?

   c. Size of sample?

   d. Representativeness of sample?

   e. Strength of generalization?

3. "The 1980 census [a survey of every household in the country] showed that the population of Mudville rose dramatically during the 1970s."
   a. Generalization?

   b. Subgroups of whole group?

   c. Size of sample?

   d. Representativeness of sample?

   e. Strength of generalization?

Write the letter of the most reasonable generalization on the line in front of each item. Explain your choice in the space provided.

_____4. Suppose you found that in your public, suburban high school, those students who do more homework also get better grades. Which of the following is the best generalization to make from this information?

    A. In your state, students who do more homework get better grades.

    B. In your school district, students who do more homework get better grades.

    C. In public, suburban high schools in the United States, students who do more homework get better grades.

    D. Students who do more homework get better grades.

Explain your choice.

_____5. Suppose you knew that Switzerland, which is a small, mountainous country, has used a strong defense (large military) to successfully avoid war. Which of the following is the best generalization to make from this information?

    A. A large military is the key to avoiding war.

    B. Small countries can use a strong defense to avoid war.

    C. Large countries can use a strong defense to avoid war.

    D. Mountainous countries can avoid war through building a strong defense.

Explain your choice.

_____6. You know that 75% of the kids in your ninth-grade homeroom like rock music best. Which of the following is the best generalization to make from this information?

    A. Most ninth-graders in your school like rock music best.

    B. Anywhere you go in the country, you'll find that most teenagers like rock music best.

    C. All ninth-grade students like rock music best.

    D. Few ninth-grade students in your school like classical music.

Explain your choice.

 © 1983, 1990 Midwest Publications • Critical Thinking Press & Software

WORKSHEET I   Identifying Unstated Assumptions — 1

What are the unstated assumptions in each of the following arguments? If you need help, look at the section on **Assumptions** in the "Guide to Critical Thinking."

1. "Why can't you study like your brother? He gets all A's in school."

2. "Beth is older than Peter, so she must be older than Marie also."

3. "Even if I have a head start running to the beach, you'll get there first."

4. "Are you sure you want to apply for that job? It requires someone with good writing skills."

5. "When I get my raise, I'm going to buy a new car."

6. "Jim, why don't you come drinking with us? You've got to learn to relax and enjoy life."

WORKSHEET J   Identifying Unstated Assumptions — 2

This four-step approach is one method for identifying unstated assumptions.

Step 1	Write out the premise. (The premise is the part of an argument that tells "why" something is true. Look for the place to put "because." What follows is the premise.)
Step 2	Find and write out the conclusion of the argument. (Look for the place to put "therefore." What follows it is the conclusion.)
Step 3	Find the unique part of the conclusion (the part that doesn't appear in the premise) and the unique part of the premise (the part that doesn't appear in the conclusion.)
Step 4	Combine the two unique parts in a sentence that starts with a general word, such as people, wars, or countries. This sentence is the unstated assumption.

 Try the four-step approach on the following claims. If you need help, look at the section on **Assumptions** in the "Guide to Critical Thinking." The first one is done for you as an example.

1. "Roger is not a football player, since he weighs only 130 pounds."
   Step 1:   "Because" he weighs only 130 pounds. (Premise)
   Step 2:   "Therefore" Roger is not a football player. (Conclusion)
   Step 3:   …weighs only 130 pounds (P)/…not a football player (C)
   Step 4:   "People" who weigh only 130 pounds are not football players.

2. Fred is definitely a good mechanic. He works for the Shell Station which is known for its fine mechanical work.
   Step 1:

   Step 2:

   Step 3:

   Step 4:

3. Sequoia is in the band and Leona isn't, so Sequoia must be a better musician.
   Step 1:

   Step 2:

   Step 3:

   Step 4:

WORSHEET K   Analyzing Historical Films

When watching a film or video interpretation of any event, consider using the following (**PIPER**) model of analysis.

P	Point of View?
I	Inferences?
P	Persuasive Techniques?
E	Evidence?
R	Relevant Information?

Use this worksheet to help you analyze historical films you watch.

1. Name of film:

2. Main point of the film:

3. **P** What is the **point of view** of the film? Was it overly favorable or critical of a particular group or individual?

4. **I** What **inferences** were made in the film? Were there parts of the film that the filmmakers must have made up because they couldn't have known this from the available evidence?

5. **P** What techniques are used in the film to **persuade** the audience to the filmmaker's point of view? Note music, camera angle, character portrayal, etc.

6. **E** What **evidence** is included to support the point of view put forth in the film? What is the source of that evidence? How strong is it?

7. **R** What **relevant information** do I know? Does it contradict or support the story presented in the film?

8. Overall, how strong are the historical arguments in this film? Is it historically accurate?

WORKSHEET L   Analyzing Historical Interpretations
Lesson _____   Interpretation _____

 Answer the following questions on each interpretation.

1. What is the main idea of this interpretation?

2. List two or three key points the author(s) use(s) to support the main idea, write any evidence given to support the point, and evaluate the evidence according to the **PROP** questions.

Key Point	Evidence that supports the point	Evaluation of Evidence
1		
2		

3. Identify and analyze one cause-and-effect argument the interpretation makes. Fill in the cause and the effect first, then complete the diagram.

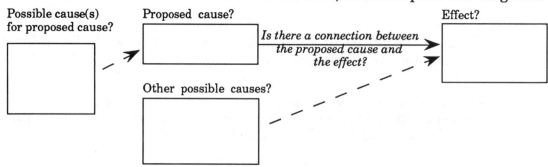

   Overall, how strong is this cause-and-effect reasoning?

4. Analyze any other aspect of the argument presented in the interpretation. For example, evaluate a generalization, comparison, or proof argument; identify an unstated assumption; note vague or emotional words that need to be defined more clearly by the author.

5. If **Relevant Information** is provided, does any of the given information affect this interpretation? If so, identify the specific information by number(s) and state the effect(s) of each on the interpretation.

6. What is your overall judgment of the interpretation? Identify its strengths and weaknesses.

UNIT 2
EXPLORATION AND COLONIES

Lesson 1: Identifying Sources

Objectives

To distinguish between supported and unsupported claims
To recognize sources of information

Teaching Ideas

You can make the lesson easier by telling students that the first sentence in each item (except #3) is the claim. When discussing the worksheet items, ask a student to give an answer to each problem, then ask if all agree with the answers given and why.

Suggested Answers

1. N

2. S [N] This is a gray area. Since the tests are technically a source, S seems to be a better answer.

3. N

4. S Postman's book is the source.

5. S Cortez's reports are the source.

6. N Although statistics are given, no source for the statistics is provided.

7. S The source is the book cited in the footnote. Point out the use of footnotes to cite sources.

8. S The published quotation is the source.

Lesson 2: Evaluating Sources

Objective

To evaluate evidence according to specific criteria

Teaching Ideas

This basic lesson provides additional guidance for students who may have difficulty determining when a source is primary or when a person has a reason to lie.

Point out that having a "reason to lie" does not necessarily mean the source is lying; it just means you cannot accept what it says without questioning it. Ask students to give reasons for their answer choice.

Suggested Answers

1. P   Terry was present (saw the purchase).
2. S   The publishing date helps determine that the authors of the book were not around when Verrazano was exploring.
3. P   A person is always a primary source to his own actions.
4. P   Although he may be a biased observer or an inaccurate reporter, deChamplain is reporting his own observations.
5. S   It is most likely that the newspaper is relying on second-hand information. If the report had been written by someone in America, it would be a primary source.
6. S   Students may need to be reminded that textbooks are nearly always secondary sources, since it is impossible for authors to have been everywhere and seen everything.
7. P   Oglethorpe is giving his own interpretation.
8. P   The papers were part of the event reported.
9. R   If Bill did steal the radio, he has a reason to say he didn't.
10. N   Unless it really happened, the colonists would be unlikely to say that they had to depend on people they ordinarily didn't like.
11. R   Smith's story makes himself look like a great fisherman—a fish story, maybe?
12. R   Penn's statement may be intended to make his colony look good.
13. N   Inanimate objects do not lie. While it is possible that someone planted the radio in Emilie's

locker or that she bought it from the thief, the presence of the stolen radio is still damaging evidence.

14. Corroborating evidence might be found in statistics on crop output per acre in colonial America; first-hand comments from colonists regarding the fertility of their own farmland; analyses of American farmland by economists or historians.

15. Go to the original source to see if you can determine what Penn means by "best"; compare the charter and laws of Pennsylvania to those of other colonies; comments by people from all colonies about which colony was "best"; comments by people from other countries, especially those who were considering emigrating; statistics concerning immigrants to various American colonies, comparing numbers of immigrants, percentage who stayed or moved to other colonies, quality of life, etc.

Lesson 3: Determining Causes and Effects

Objectives

To distinguish between causes and effects
To consider possible causes other than or in addition to the cause proposed in an argument

Teaching Ideas
PREPARATION

Have students read the introductory section on causal reasoning in the "Guide to Critical Thinking." Also, use the introductory exercise (Worksheet E) for this skill if you have not already done so.

USING THE WORKSHEET

Ask the students to complete the first section (1–8) individually then discuss their answers in groups of 2 or 3. If you use this same procedure for the final section, discuss responses to each problem set (i.e., Grades in School) before students go to the next set. In this way students should have a good idea of how to do the last set by the time they get to it.

EXTENDING ACTIVITIES

Encourage students to bring their own knowledge (relevant information) to bear on causal claims. Remind them, however, that they should be able to state the source of their information. They might also need to be reminded to evaluate those sources before accepting the information as strong support for their contention.

Suggested Answers

1. [E]
2. [C]

3. C   This is the reason she tried out for the team.
4. E   "So" indicates the effect.

5. E
6. C   "Because" indicates cause rather than effect.

7. C
8. E   "Led to" indicates an effect.

9. Students should note a number of other possible reasons for Willie's bad grades.

10. There are other causes that contribute to becoming a good athlete, such as speed, agility, diet, and determination.

11. Students should notice that some factors are not mentioned in the argument, one important one being "curiosity."

Lesson 4: Evaluating Cause-and-Effect Relationships

Objectives

To recognize and evaluate the strength of specific cause-and-effect relationships

Teaching Ideas

PREPARATION

To make sure students understand the elements involved in causal reasoning, use the "Guide to Critical Thinking" and introductory Worksheet E.

USING THE WORKSHEET

Have students answer items 1 and 2 individually and discuss their answers with the class. They may then work in pairs on the remaining questions.

Suggested Answers

1. R Other things will also make a car stop; and fuel gauges are sometimes stuck or broken.

2. R Although there may be a relationship, no reason is given in this statement.

3. W This should prove to be an interesting discussion!

4. S This presents the same argument as item 2, but includes an explanation of how cigarette smoking causes lung cancer.

5. R The argument (connection) is reasonable, but no supporting explanation is presented. There could have been other reasons for the decline in Indian population—they could have been killed or left the country.

6. W This is debatable, for R is also possible. The argument against R is that, although many other plants are also easy to plant and cultivate, the Virginia colonists didn't plant those. The argument presented does not, therefore, give a very strong reason.

7. W It is equally likely that they intermarried with them because they got along with them, i.e., intermarriage was the effect, not the cause.

8. S This includes an explanation—missing from item 5—of how and why the diseases killed the Indians. Historians are supposed to explain how the cause led to the effect.

9. S This connects the land problem through the anger to the war (effect). The connection could be much more detailed, however, so R is also a reasonable answer.

Lesson 5: Recognizing and Assessing Cause-and-Effect Reasoning

Objectives

To identify causes and effects in given arguments
To assess the strength of a cause-effect relationship
To encourage students to think of alternative causes

Teaching Ideas

PREPARATION

This lesson is more difficult than Lessons 3 and 4, which break the skill of evaluating cause-and-effect reasoning into component parts: identifying which is the cause and which the effect; assessing the strength of the connection; thinking of possible alternative causes. If you have done Lessons 3 and 4 with your students, they should have no difficulty with this lesson, since they have already done each of the above subskills.

USING THE WORKSHEET

Have the students do the first problem in each section, then discuss their answers before they proceed with the other problems. The second set of questions in this lesson asks students to do a complete analysis of cause-and-effect reasoning.

Suggested Answers

1. C   CAUSE: invention of printing press

   CONNECTIONS: increase in number and decrease in cost of books stimulated desire to read; spread ideas of Renaissance; aroused interest in distant lands

   EFFECT: exploration

2. N   Makes no statement of either causes or effects of their decisions.

3. N   Provides no explanation of why they used such canoes or the results of such use.

4. C   CAUSE: failure of Spanish government to encourage settlement in California

   EFFECT: small Spanish population in California in 1804

5. N   Gives no explanation of why he continued to think he was in Asia.

6. N   Provides no explanation of why the French got along better.

7. This argument exposes students to the reasoning falacy of "correlation as cause." Just because A is related to B doesn't mean A caused B. Maybe B caused A or, as in this case, C (another factor) may have caused both B and A.

[7.]

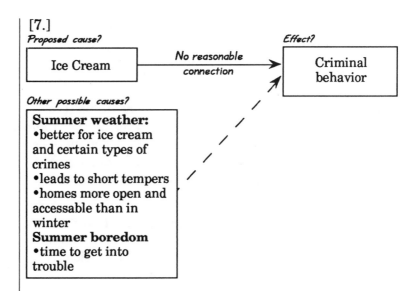

8. You can make this problem easier by asking, before students do the problem, "What are some things that cause the decline of a country or empire?"

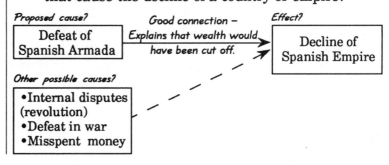

Lesson 6: Evaluating Evidence About the Colonies

Objective

To apply criteria when evaluating historical evidence

Teaching Ideas

NOTE

This is a more difficult lesson on evaluating evidence (or sources of information) than Lesson 2. In this lesson the students may learn more criteria for evaluating evidence and learn it more quickly, but some students may be confused on some criteria. Lesson 2 may be helpful for those students.

PREPARATION

You might want to focus on the four main criteria for evidence evaluation (explained in the Evidence section of the "Guide to Critical Thinking" and in Introductory Worksheets B, C, and D).

USING THE WORKSHEET

Argument 2 can be used to introduce students to other possible criteria for evaluating evidence (see below).

EXTENDING ACTIVITY

After the class discusses student answers, ask students how they might further check on these pieces of evidence. Emphasize verification processes, especially those using primary sources. Some students might wish to do, within their available resources, verification research on the topics.

Suggested Answers

STRENGTHS

1. [John Smith]
   - It is a primary source; Smith is writing of his own experiences.

WEAKNESSES

   - He has a reason to lie; he's trying to make himself look good.

   - Smith cites no other evidence supporting his claim.

   - This was written sixteen years after the event; a lot can be forgotten in that length of time.

   - It is a public statement, meant to be read by other people and intended to influence those readers.

     [You might want to point out that most people believe that John Smith did, in fact, hold Jamestown together during 1608–1609. Nevertheless, this evidence by itself is not very strong.]

2. [Christopher Columbus]

STRENGTHS

   - It is a primary source, written by a participant in the event.

(STRENGTHS)

- Columbus may have thought few people, if any, would read his journal, so he may have been more honest.

- It was written the same day as the event.

- He has no obvious reason to lie.

WEAKNESSES

- His "frame of reference"—a European meeting "uncivilized" natives—might lead him to distort what he sees.

- He might have expected that someone would read his journal sometime, so he wouldn't want to make himself look bad; the journal may have been his record of the voyage intended to be given to the King and Queen of Spain, who had paid for his trip.

- There is no other evidence given to support the stated observations.

- He makes judgments about the natives based on his unconscious assumptions as a European; e.g., if they are naked, they must be very poor.

  Discussion of this item may well lead into extended criteria. Values and assumptions play an important role in this excerpt. Encourage students to go beyond the **PROP** criteria by asking questions such as, "What did Columbus seem to think of the Salvadorian Indians? What makes you think he felt that way? Do you think his beliefs were accurate? Why or why not?"

3. [Rebecca Gruver]

STRENGTHS

- Other historians support her point of view.

- As a historian she has some authority to make such judgments.

- She has no obvious reason to lie.

WEAKNESSES

- This is a secondary source, since an author writing in 1972 would not have been a first-hand observer of the leadership qualities of William Penn in the 1600s.

- A history book is a public statement meant to be read by others, especially students of history (her peers). She might want to agree with famous historians to make herself look good.

Lesson 7: What Happened to Roanoke?

Objective

To relate relevant information to hypotheses
To identify and evaluate evidence
To recognize unstated assumptions

Teaching Ideas

PREPARATION

The brainstorming question, "List reasons that a colony in America in the 1500s might fail and disappear," is important to the lesson in that it emphasizes the idea that it is helpful to scan our previous knowledge to see what might be relevant to a given topic.

USING THE WORKSHEETS

When students have generated several theories, ask them to read the background section. You might wish to ask some factual questions to make sure they understand the main points; e.g., "Where is Roanoke?" "Who is John White?" "Why did he leave the colony?" "What message did the colonists leave?" Give students time to add theories to their original list at this point, also.

Ask students to share and discuss their responses to the question, and list the suggested theories on the chalkboard. If students suggest enough alternatives to satisfy you, have them read the Relevant Information (RI) and study the map. Ask them to explain if or how this new information affects their theories.

ENABLING ACTIVITY

If you do not think students have generated enough reasonable theories, ask them to read the theories on the optional worksheet **Evaluating Theories About Roanoke**, then go on to the step involving the Relevant Information and the map.

EXTENDING THE LESSON

Focus the objective on evidence by asking students to determine which of the Relevant Information items would be considered evidence (i.e., source given) and which would not. Extend the activity by asking students to evaluate one piece of evidence.

Help students recognize assumptions by asking:

- "How many of you assumed the Roanoke colonists stayed together as a group?"

  (Most students will not recognize that assumption until they have read RI 10.)

- "How many of you assumed that the Roanoke colonists were the only Englishmen who could have intermarried with the Croatoan Indians?"

  (It is possible that other Englishmen were shipwrecked near Croatoan and lived with the

Indians; or the seventeen men left by the supply ship could have been responsible for the intermarriages. Many Englishmen of the time had similar last names.)

Suggested Answers

RELATING RELEVANT INFORMATION (RI) TO THEORIES: WORKSHEET

Theory A

- Relevant Information (RI) 3 weakens this theory. The lack of any record for something as important as a military attack indicates that such an attack probably didn't take place.

- If colonists were killed where were the bodies? Why was there no sign of a battle? (It is possible, however, that the Spanish buried the bodies and covered up the evidence of an attack.)

- If the colonists were attacked or in danger, why didn't they put a cross on a tree?

- If they were under attack, why did they write CROATOAN on the tree?

Theory B

- RI 8 supports the possibility of boats, either going to sea or sailing within the cape area, being sunk.

- RI 10 weakens this theory. Although the colonists may have sailed quite a distance along the coast to move inland, they would always have been at least fairly close to land. Thus, even if a boat sank it is unlikely that no one would have made it to shore.

- RI 10 and 11 indicate that it is unlikely that all the colonists would have been at sea at the same time. This decreases the likelihood that all the colonists were killed at sea, since it would have taken two or three separate shipwrecks to kill everyone.

Theory C

- RI 2 and 5 indicate that Powhatan killed them, although 5 does not mention the colony by name.

- RI 6 indicates that at least one Englishman believed the colonists were in the Chesapeake area in 1603.

- RI 9 says that the Chesapeakes had met some of the colonists previously and were friendly toward them. This suggests that the colonists could have gone to the Indians for aid or support and would have been favorably received.

- RI 10 supports the theory by indicating that the colonists considered moving inland even before White left for England.

- One problem with the theory is the distance (about 50 miles) from Roanoke to Skicoac. It would have been difficult for such a large number of colonists to travel that far, probably partly over land, and transport all of their possessions.

Theory D

- RI 1 shows that the colonists had met and established a relationship with at least some members of the Croatoan tribe.

- RI 4 shows that some people in England believed there were Englishmen on Croatoan—although it is possible that they came from a group other than those on Roanoke.

- RI 7 is strong evidence. Although it is possible that other Englishmen intermarried with the Croatoans, the message on the tree and the same last names make it seem highly probable that at least some of the Roanoke colonists ended up on Croatoan Island.

Theory E

- No information is offered to support or refute this theory. You might decide not to use this theory, or you might want to use and discuss it. How do "mystery theories" such as this compare with the more "mainstream" historical theories?

Theory F

- RI 2 and 5 support this theory. Weaknesses are the same as the unanswered questions listed under Theory A.

IDENTIFYING EVIDENCE

Relevant Information items which include sources and should be considered evidence are 2, 4, 5, 7, and 9.

EVALUATING EVIDENCE

If necessary, remind students of the **PROP** method of evaluating evidence.

RI 2 **P**—This is a secondary source; Strachey was not present in Roanoke.

R—Neither Strachey nor the king has an obvious reason to lie.

O—No supporting evidence is given.

P—The book is a public statement.

Although the book was written within a year or two of the alleged massacre, an eyewitness account, or at least some supporting evidence of the event, would be preferred.

RI 4 **P**—The instructions are a primary source.

R—There is no apparent reason for the instructions to lie or mislead, unless the English knew they were going to be captured by the Spanish and wrote the instructions to intentionally mislead their captors.

O—There is no other supporting evidence given.

P—It is a public source, meant to be read by the English ship's officers.

The instructions written in England are a source, but not a specific source; use of the word "supposedly" weakens the evidence.

RI 5 **P**—This is a secondary (actually tertiary) source; the author was not present at either the "murder" or the retelling of the story.

R—There is no obvious reason for the author to intentionally lie. The problem is with the authenticity of third-hand information.

O—No supporting evidence is given.

P—It is a public statement.

RI 7 **P**—The hunters are a primary source.

R—There is no reason for the hunters to lie, unless they were seeking fame.

O—Since there was more than one hunter, their evidence supports each other; no additional support is given from other sources, however.

P—The source is a public statement.

A written record of their testimony would be a better source of evidence; report borders on rumor.

RI 9 **P**—The colonists are primary sources about staying with the Indians.

R—They had no reason to lie, unless they wanted to make the Indians look good.

O—They support each other's evidence.

P—It is public evidence.

RECOGNIZING
UNSTATED ASSUMPTIONS

Assumptions which students may make, and which you may point out, include:

- The colonists stayed as a group.
- The colonists all had the same fate.
- The Roanoke Colonists were the only Englishmen who had contact with the Indians up to 1608 (the Jamestown Settlement).
- All Indians had the same view of the colonists.

Lesson 8: Did Pocahontas Really Rescue Captain John Smith?

Objectives

To identify and evaluate evidence
To identify hypotheses
To relate relevant information to hypotheses

Teaching Ideas

Note

This lesson focuses on the use of evidence to support historical hypotheses (interpretations). The conflicting nature of the evidence and claims should lead to lively class discussions and some good thinking.

Using the Worksheet

With this in mind it is recommended that you **NOT** use the worksheet included in the lesson. The worksheet is a bit too structured. You might, however, refer to the worksheet for questions to help guide class discussion.

Some students and classes, on the other hand, may need this more structured format—which is why it is included.

Optional Worksheet or Discussion Guides

You might want to have the whole class turn to the section on **Evidence** in the "Guide to Critical Thinking." If you have done an evidence problem already, remind students of the **PROP** criteria for judging evidence. Refer them to the poster or to that section in their notebooks.

Suggested Analysis

In support of Interpretation A, students could note that:

- Since Pocahontas had become famous, Smith had a motive for making up the story.

- Other quotations from Smith show that he had a tendency to lie or exaggerate.

- Smith didn't mention the rescue in his first account of that time. Most people would have mentioned such a significant event.

- The similarity between his story and the De Soto story of 1607 (RI 3) tends to discredit one or both stories.

- It is highly improbable that Smith was rescued so frequently by pretty women.

- Raphe Hamor failed to mention the incident in 1615 (RI 1).

- Nothing is provided in Interpretation B to show the rescue took place; that interpretation only attempts to prove that Smith was not generally a liar.

In support of Interpretation B, students could note that:

- Smith's original manuscript of *True Relation* might have mentioned the rescue, but it was edited out.

- Smith is actually an accurate reporter, just a poor speller.
- Smith and others were attacked by Powhatan, so it's possible the Indians were hostile to him (RI 2).

Suggested Answers

OPTIONAL WORKSHEET
OR DISCUSSION GUIDES

Interpretation A

1. D

2. Many could be selected. In Endnote 1, for example, *True Relation* is a primary source (P) with no obvious reason to lie (R). There is no other evidence (O) that the rescue didn't take place, and it is public (P).

   You may wish to point out the endnote numbers. Explain that they usually refer to evidence in support of an argument or interpretation. Be certain that students do not confuse these with the paragraph numbers at the beginning of each paragraph.

   Ask students to explain why their choice is evidence.

   - Is it a statement by a witness, a written document, or an object?
   - Does it show the source?

   This may have to be repeated several times before students remember the process for separating evidence from statements or assertions.

3. Consistency of a witness. You can remind students of the story about the boy who cried wolf. Do students tend to believe people who lie to them all the time? Should they?

4. These stories may indicate that Smith really liked the idea of being rescued by women and that he made up the Pocahontas story, too. Ask the students if they think it is realistic for one person to be rescued by beautiful women so many times—a theoretical question, to be sure!

Interpretation B

5. The main point of this interpretation is that Pocahontas probably did rescue John Smith. "Smith was not a liar" is an argument to prove the main point.

6. Examples of evidence in this interpretation include *True Relation* (see answer to question 2) and Smith's accounts of the wars with the Turks.

7. It offers corroboration (other evidence saying the same thing) for Smith's story of what happened.

General Questions

8. Some of the details are different; e.g., Powhatan lying down in the first, but seated in the second; different spelling of place name; differing report of content of conversation with Powhatan. This may show inaccurate reporting by Smith, although the discrepancies seem minor.

9. RI 1 Tends to show the rescue did not take place. Why wouldn't someone who knew about such a significant event as the rescue report it?

    RI 2 Tends to show the rescue did take place. If this is indeed the same incident (which is unclear), it casts doubt on Smith's report in *True Relation*. If the Indians killed two men who were with Smith, why would they be friendly toward him? It is more likely the Indians were ready to kill him, too, as reported in *Generall Historie*.

    RI 3 Tends to show the rescue did not take place. Since this story appeared after *True Relation* but before *Generall Historie*, it supports the hypothesis that Smith may have made up the rescue story after hearing, and liking, this one.

10. Sources might include other primary accounts of Jamestown or Pocahontas or a check on the veracity of other accounts by Smith. If students mention books or texts that are not primary sources, it will help them realize the problem if you ask, "Where did the authors get their information?"

Lesson 9: How Did Immigration to Colonial Maryland Affect the Lives of Women?

Objectives

To use and assess cause-and-effect reasoning
To evaluate samples and generalizations

Teaching Ideas
PREPARATION

Have the students look at the section on Cause-and-Effect Reasoning in the "Guide to Critical Thinking" if they have difficulty with causal predictions.

The second worksheet in this lesson focuses student attention on the hazards of extending a generalization from a sample. You might want to have them read the section on Generalization in the "Guide to Critical Thinking" and do the introductory lesson (Worksheet H, pages 44–46, *Teacher's Guide*) on samples and generalization.

On the other hand, doing this lesson with no preparation may have greater impact on students. Having overgeneralized in this lesson, students may internalize the warning against overgeneralizing in the future.

USING THE WORKSHEETS

The sections on projecting effects of conditions in Maryland emphasizes generating ideas for possible effects then following these ideas further by inferring possible effects of those effects. Focus the class on evaluating their causal predictions by asking two questions:

- **How** would this condition lead to that effect? **How** are the two things connected? (For example, how might being away from their relatives give women more "bargaining power" with their husbands?)

- **Could** this condition lead to some other, more important effect that would cancel out your predicted effect? (For example, could being away from their relatives in any way weaken a woman's position in regard to her husband?)

Some information in this lesson is tentative and needs further research. The worksheet's focus, however, is on how to project or extend personal knowledge, tentative though it may be, into new areas. You might want to discuss with the class the value—and danger—of accepting (stipulating) tentative claims for the sake of the particular argument.

The true-false questions serve to shift the focus of the class from causal reasoning to sample reasoning.

Suggested Answers

1. [Effects on women's lives of immigration to Maryland in the 1600s.]

Effect	Effects of Effect
RI 6 Increase in social freedom (moved away from relatives)	Increase in out-of-wedlock pregnancies
RI 7 Women had more choices among marriage partners	Happier marriages Marriages not as male-dominated
RI 8 Later marriages (older when married)	Fewer children
RI 9 Women tended to outlive their first husbands (see RI 11)	Increase in number of second marriages
Children were not adults when their fathers died (see RI 12)	Widows rather than grown sons inherited estates; more children raised by step-fathers
RI 10 Second-generation Marylanders (born in Maryland) married at an earlier age than their parents had.	Increase in number of children (due to longer marriages)
RI 11 Increase in number of second or third marriages for women	Increase in number of children borne by a woman; increase in number of children raised by step-father
Increase in females who had no way to support their families.	Death of women and/or fatherless children by starvation or exposure
RI 12 Children of marriages were still too young to assume adult responsibilities	Increase in second marriages and in marriages of convenience
RI 13 More children conceived to make up for high mortality rate	Increase in population and in infant mortality rate
Low rate of population growth among immigrants	Most increases in population came from new immigration, not from children

2. [Effects and extended effects of earlier marriages of immigrants' daughters.]

Effect	Effects of Effect	Further Effects
Increase in number of children born	Increased number survived to adulthood	Extended family begins again
	Greater balance between numbers of men and women	Women had less choice in marriage partners
	Women died at an earlier age due to complications of pregnancies and childbirth	Men, left with young families to care for, married women younger than themselves
		Increased imbalance between numbers of men and women of marriageable age
Men usually had some adult children by the time they died.	Inheritance passed to adult sons rather than to widow	Women lost the power to control their own lives
	Adults exercised more social control over lives of their children	Fewer out-of-wedlock pregnancies

Note: The important point in deciding how far to generalize (extend a sample) is in determining to what extent the sample represents the whole group. Remind skeptical students that television ratings and presidential polls, although based on very small samples (generally about 1200 people), are usually so representative of the whole group that they are reliable.

3. This could be an overgeneralization. Although the statement may be true, it cannot be generalized from the given information with "reasonable confidence." It is important to note that immigrants to New England more frequently came in family groups (social control and less imbalance between numbers of men and women), had longer life expectancies (fathers more likely to give property to adult sons,

fewer second marriages, etc.), and had more children (population expansion by reproduction) than did immigrants to Maryland.

4. For this to be true, students would need to know more about living conditions all over the world in the 1600s. There are just too many factors involved—diseases, urbanization, weather, and wars, to name a few—to generalize about statistics on world-wide life expectancy.

5. T

    Since this statement is restricted to Maryland, and since it reflects information students have been given, it is not an extension of the sample and is likely to be true.

6. Since conditions in the general Chesapeake Region tended to be similar to those in Maryland (low life expectancy, late marriage, more men than women, etc.), this statement may be true. A few sources of supporting information on conditions in Virginia would add strength to the argument.

7. T

    Since this statement is restricted to Maryland, and since it reflects information students have been given, it is not an extension of the sample and is likely to be true.

Lesson 10: What Really Caused the Salem Witch Hysteria?

Objectives

To evaluate historical evidence
To relate relevant information to hypotheses
To assess the strength of cause-and-effect reasoning
To evaluate the validity of generalizations

Teaching Ideas

NOTE

This interesting problem should take at least three class periods to analyze and evaluate. If you have less time, use only three or four of the interpretations.

The following materials comprise the lesson.

Item	Description/Main Idea
Information	Background / Relevant Information (RI)
Glossary of Terms	Defines terms peculiar to the times or events
Figure 3	Map of Salem Area
Figure 4	Map showing some locations of accused witch's households
Time Line	Chronology of events
Afflicted & Accused	Information about those on both sides of the trials
Interpretation A	"Clergy were responsible"
Interpretation B	"Girls were bored and liked the attention"
Interpretation C	"Caused by ergot poisoning"
Interpretation D	"Caused by belief in and practice of witchcraft"
Interpretation E	"Caused by economic and religious divisions within Salem Village"
Interpretation F	"Society picking on outcasts"
Interpretation G	"Caused by general unrest in the colony"
Worksheet L	For analyzing interpretations

INTRODUCING THE LESSON	An important focus of this lesson is causation: What caused the hysteria? Introduce the lesson by asking students "Why do people sometimes act strangely? Why might a whole town begin to act strangely and end up killing some people?" These two brainstorming questions will help students think of a variety of possible causes before encountering causes proposed in the interpretations. You could discuss these briefly or you could list their answers on the chalkboard. (Note that this strategy was also used in Lesson 3.)
USING THE INFORMATION	Make sure students read and understand the overview (especially the Background Information and the maps) before proceeding with the interpretations. Go over the maps and, if necessary, the time line, glossary, and information on the afflicted and the accused. All of these together should give the students a good idea of the general situation in the Salem area in 1692.
	Students may read the Relevant Information either before they read the interpretations or after they have made some judgments about them. The latter strategy would clarify the concept of history as a process of interpretation and reinterpretation.
USING THE INTERPRETATIONS	Interpretations A and B provide a more narrative style, although each view clearly proposes a primary cause of the hysteria. The other interpretations are analytical, providing a thesis and evidence to support it. It might be helpful to point out the two interpretation styles to students, emphasizing that even narrative histories have a particular point of view, a clear argument. Where endnotes are used, they are as given in the original sources. Encourage students to consider them.
	The interpretations themselves could be discussed in several ways. Students could read them all, then decide which they think is the best interpretation and why. Class discussion should then focus on claims and counterclaims, probing for the strengths and weaknesses of each viewpoint. In such a discussion, encourage students to question the evidence, the causal reasoning, and other aspects of each view.
	A second methodology is to have students defend particular interpretations in a debate on the witch trials.
	A third method is to have students analyze the interpretations in small groups. Each group would then report to the full class on which viewpoint it thinks is strongest and why.

SUPPLEMENTAL ACTIVITIES

A fourth strategy is to have students use copies of Worksheet L (p. 50, *Teacher's Guide*) for the interpretations. (Even if you don't have students use the worksheet, you may want to refer to it for questions you might ask.)

Several films, such as *The Witches of Salem* (rental, Learning Corporation of America) and *Three Sovereigns for Sarah* (rental, Station WGBH, Boston),[1] could be used with this lesson. Films can be approached in several ways.

1. Ask the students:
   - How do films differ from written arguments?
   - Do films have a point of view?
   - Do films present arguments?
   - How do filmmakers persuade viewers to their points of view? What techniques do they use?
   - How do films make use of evidence?

2. Use the questions from Worksheet K ("Analyzing Historical Films," page 50, *Teacher's Guide*) or ask students to complete the worksheet.

If only one film is used, students are likely to agree with it even though weaknesses in the film are pointed out to them. *The Witches of Salem* has a number of weaknesses.

1. There is no evidence that Bridget Bishop wore low-cut (sexy) dresses; only that she wore clothing that did not fit her social class.

2. John Proctor was in his 50s in 1692. It is unlikely that any of the girls would have been infatuated with him.

3. The opinion that the girls were faking, expressed as a fact in the film, is open to question.

4. The housing shown is from the early 1600s, rather than the late 1600s.

5. Some characters in the film represent multiple people from the actual trials. For example, John Proctor says some things that he said, some things that George Burroughs said, and some things about which there is no evidence anyone said.

Three Sovereigns for Sarah may be too long (three hours) for classroom use, although parts of it could be shown. The film centers on three sisters—Sarah Cloyse, Mary Esty, and Rebecca Nurse—who were among the accused.

---

[1] Both films are also available on videotape and can be purchased from Social Studies School Service.

Although it adheres to the historical record better than *The Witches of Salem*, it draws inferences at some points.

1. There is little historical evidence regarding exactly what took place when the girls first met at Reverend Parris's home in the winter of 1691–1692, thus most of what is shown in the film is conjecture on that point.

2. There is evidence that Reverend Parris and others asked the girls who was afflicting them, but no evidence that Reverend Parris or anyone else suggested particular names.

3. There is no evidence that Sarah Cloyse argued her case before three magistrates or that she had a map showing conflict in the village. The map idea is, in fact, a theory (Interpretation E) proposed by two historians.

Suggested Analyses

Interpretation A

MAIN IDEA

Clergy were primarily responsible for the witch hysteria.

KEY POINTS AND EVIDENCE

(Paragraph numbers in parentheses):

(2) *The ministers suggested the names of the witches.* Only one name is mentioned in the interpretation. No evidence is offered to support the point.

(4–5) *Several ministers (Lawson and Parris) preached sermons which stressed the Devil and thus kept the hysteria going.* Although Lawson's sermon is quoted in the source cited in endnote 1 and sounds like a good piece of evidence, a longer quotation would provide more context. The second quotation (Parris's) is very damaging to Parris. Since Calef lived in Boston rather than Salem, however, it is unlikely that he heard the sermon personally. Also, Calef was opposed to the trials, so he is not objective. Since it is unclear if endnote 3 really proves that Reverend Ballard asked Ann Putnam, Jr. to come to Andover, it is hard to evaluate that claim. It would be easy, however, to verify if the hysteria spread to Andover.

(6) *The ministers' letter recommended vigorous prosecution of the witches.* However, the letter was apparently moderate in other areas. The actual letter is reprinted in the cited source, which makes it a primary source.

(6) *Cotton Mather got the hanging of Burroughs to proceed.* The evidence is very damaging to

Mather, but he is only one minister. Although it is impossible to tell if the source is primary or secondary, Calef was a known biased observer.

(7) *The ministers used the witch hysteria to try to hold on to power.* There is no evidence to support this contention.

CAUSAL
REASONING

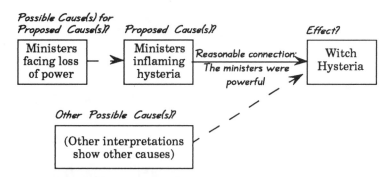

Overall judgment: Except for the sermon by Parris, the evidence that the ministers inflamed the hysteria is all based on Calef, a biased source. More evidence that the ministers were losing power, that people listened to what the ministers were saying, and that they actually said things that inflamed the hysteria is needed.

OTHER
ASPECTS

Generalization (sample): This interpretation mentions many local ministers (Parris, Noyes, Hale, Ballard, Lawson), but fails to show that each one inflamed the hysteria.

RELEVANT
INFORMATION

RI 6, 11, and 12 tend to show that the ministers were not so in favor of the Trials as Interpretation A argues.

Interpretation B

MAIN IDEA

The witchcraft hysteria started because the afflicted girls craved attention and continued because adults believed the girls.

KEY POINTS
AND EVIDENCE

(1) *The girls were bored and needed an outlet for their natural emotional energy.* No evidence given.

(3) *The girls became important people in the village.* No evidence is given supporting their importance or popularity.

(4) *The girls reversed several decisions.* The evidence on Mary Esty is primary, from the examination testimony. The evidence regarding Rebecca Nurse is from a biased source (Calef), and it is unclear whether Calef was present at the Nurse trial.

(5) *The girls couldn't have backed out.* No evidence is given.

(6) *Accusers who tried to recant were not believed.* On both Mary Warren and Sarah Churchill, the evidence is primary.

(8) *The girls were faking.* No evidence is presented, but the information that the girls suffered no fits after the trials is persuasive.

CAUSAL
REASONING

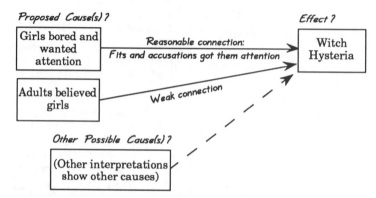

Overall judgment: Several possible questions are left unanswered by this causal reasoning. Why didn't the girls stop accusing after awhile and just say "We've caught all the witches"? How did the girls originally know they would get attention from their fits? What caused the adults to believe the girls?

OTHER
ASPECTS

Unstated assumptions: The author of this interpretation assumes that all of the accused were innocent of witchcraft; for example, he assumes that Tituba was lying when she confessed. Additionally, he assumes that all of the accusers made up their symptoms.

RELEVANT
INFORMATION

RI 24, 25, 27, and 28 tend to cast doubts on the part of this theory that says the girls were faking. RI 16, 17, 18, 20, and 22 tend to support the contention that the girls were faking.

Interpretation C

MAIN IDEA

Ergot poisoning was the main cause of the Salem witch hysteria.

KEY POINTS
AND EVIDENCE

(3) *The time of year and the people afflicted (girls) fit with ergot poisoning.* No evidence given.

(4) *The weather was right for ergot growth.* The tree rings and diaries support the points about the weather well, but no evidence is cited relating such weather to growth of ergot fungus.

(5–6) *The afflicted people were from or near farms where their rye was highly likely to be infected with ergot.* No source is given for the information.

(7) *Symptoms of the afflicted girls were the same as those of ergot poisoning.* The source, *Ergot Alkaloids*, is a primary source if these authors observed the effects of ergot. However, would the symptoms today by the same as those in 1690?

Note: All of the above points are circumstantial; that is they **allow** for ergot to be the cause but they don't show it to be the cause.

CAUSAL
REASONING

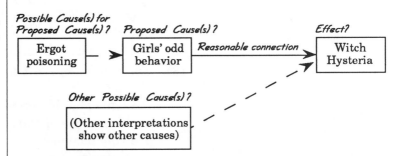

Overall judgment: The proposed cause would explain the girls' odd behavior but not the adults' allowing it to turn into full-scale hysteria.

OTHER
ASPECTS

Assumption: At the end of paragraph 6, the author of Interpretation C assumes that land suitable for rye cultivation was used to grow rye.

RELEVANT
INFORMATION

RI 29, 30, and 31 weaken this interpretation considerably. Also, if students check the ages of the afflicted girls, they will note that only one of the afflicted was under ten years of age, and only two others were between the ages of ten and fifteen. This weakens the argument in paragraph 2 of the interpretation.

Interpretation D

MAIN IDEA

Belief in and practice of witchcraft was the key cause of the Salem witch trials. (NOTE: The author does not seem to be arguing that the accused were guilty and therefore rightfully hanged. Rather the argument is that the belief in and actual practice of witchcraft made it very real to the villagers, thus leading to the hysteria.)

KEY POINTS
AND EVIDENCE

(2–5) *Witchcraft was practiced and believed in Salem.* The evidence from the confessions is tricky since the confessors may have believed they could avoid hanging by confessing. On the other hand, why did they tell much more than they had to?

The puppets do not seem damaging to Bridget Bishop, except that they were in a house where she had lived. That certainly does not constitute proof that they were her puppets, and there is no information regarding the men who testified that they had found the puppets in her home. They may have had a reason to lie.

Although the evidence regarding Margaret Rule is impressive, it is only one case.

(6–7) *The girls were not faking; they were medically hysterical.* The evidence by John Hale is strong (primary, no apparent reason to lie). One weakness is that Reverend Hale's belief in witches and the Devil may have affected his point of view and prevented him from recognizing faking.

(8) *The ministers tried to control the hysteria from the beginning.* The evidence is reasonable, but students should notice that provocative sermons, such as those of Parris and Noyes, for example, are conspicuously absent. (This is the fallacy of *special pleading*, as described in the "Guide to Critical Thinking. In this case, the author includes only those ministerial actions intended to stop the hysteria, leaving out any reference to actions that might have inflamed the hysteria.)

CAUSAL
REASONING

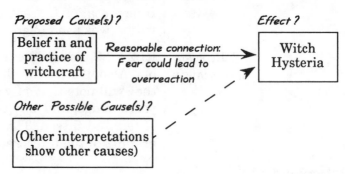

Overall judgment: The connection seems reasonable in explaining both the accusations ("These afflictions are the Devil's work") and the adults' accepting behavior toward the afflicted girls.

OTHER
ASPECTS

Generalization (sample): The author claims that since several people confessed to witchcraft, several others accused people of witchcraft, and still others claimed they witnessed levitation, **most** citizens of Salem at the time either believed in or practiced witchcraft. The generalization would have been more reliable if more of the population had been taken into consideration. The sample of those accused who confessed seems reasonable. The problem, as explained above, was with the confessions.

Assumption (paragraph 3): Someone who can make no reasonable reply to a charge must be guilty.

RELEVANT INFORMATION

RI 6, 9, 11, 12, 20, 23, 24, 25, 26, 27, and 28 support this interpretation. RI 16, 17, 18, and 22 cast doubts on it.

Interpretation E

MAIN IDEA

Economic and religious divisions and disputes within Salem Village were the key causes of the witch hysteria.

KEY POINTS AND EVIDENCE

(4–6) *Citizens of Salem Village were divided on many issues, including the issue of independence from Salem Town.* No source is given to support the claims.

(9) *The locations of accusers and defenders in the witchcraft trials follow other divisions within the area.* No sources are given for the map. Although the list of pro- and anti-Parris petition signers is from a primary source, these petitions were signed after the trials were over. Thus, they may have been a result rather than a cause of the hysteria. For example, a person who initially looked favorably upon Reverend Parris may have become sufficiently upset by the trials to sign the anti-Parris petition when the trials were over.

(10) *Several of the afflicted came from the households of Reverend Parris and Thomas Putnam, two people heavily involved in the decision to break away from Salem Village.* There is no source of evidence given, but this information could easily be checked.

CAUSAL REASONING

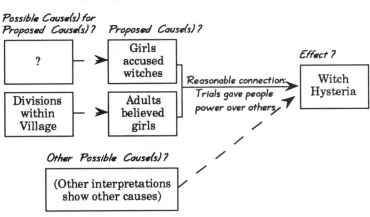

Overall judgment: This interpretation offers a reasonable rationale for why adults believed the afflicted girls but not why the girls accused. The 82% figure mentioned in paragraph 8, however, seems to undercut the argument that internal disputes were the key to the witch hunts.

OTHER ASPECTS

Reasoning by Proof: The evidence is presented in an attempt to show that there were disputes. Even if this is assumed to be true, there is no evidence to show that the disputes caused the accusations or influenced particular accusations.

RELEVANT INFORMATION

RI 3, 4, and 8 support this interpretation; RI 10 and 14 raise questions about it.

Interpretation F

MAIN IDEA

The witch hysteria was an attempt to control the social behavior and force conformity on the people.

KEY POINTS AND EVIDENCE

(1) *All of the accused were outcasts from society.* Although the three people cited may (or may not) have been social outcasts, no source is given to support the point.

(2) *Society gained because the trials showed people the limits of antisocial or deviant behavior.* No evidence is given.

CAUSAL REASONING

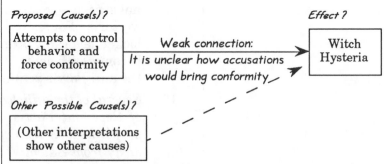

Overall judgment: No evidence is presented to show that people intended to control such behavior.

OTHER ASPECTS

Generalization: The author uses three examples to generalize about all the accused (several hundred). There should be a much larger sample, as this sample of three is quite likely not representative.

RELEVANT INFORMATION

RI 10 and 13 weaken this view.

Interpretation G

MAIN IDEA

Unstable political and religious conditions led to the original accusations and the witch hysteria.

KEY POINTS AND EVIDENCE

(2) *Conditions in 1692 caused instability.* Although many examples are given, the author provides no evidence to support this claim.

(3) *Stress from disease, attack, arguments, and the weather added to the unstable conditions.* No evidence is given.

CAUSAL
REASONING

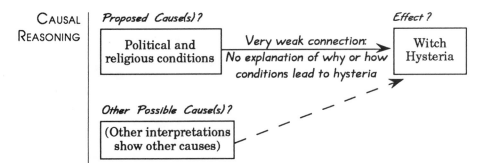

Overall judgment: No real cause is proposed, but rather conditions of the time. Since many of these conditions existed throughout the colonies in the 1600s, it is hard to see how they could be considered causes in the same way that, say, clinical hysteria caused the episode. For example, when you fall down, you might say, "I tripped"; you would not be likely to say, "Gravity (a condition) pulled me down." Also, the author never explains what the "spark" (paragraph 4) was that finally caused the explosion.

OTHER
ASPECTS

Assumption: The author assumes that the people of Massachusetts were so upset by the charter question that it affected their everyday lives. The author also assumes that rebellions in other colonies had a significant effect on the people of Massachusetts.

RELEVANT INFORMATION

None of the Relevant Information relates to this view.

UNIT 3
THE AMERICAN REVOLUTION

Lesson 11: Evaluating Evidence: Strengths and Weaknesses

Objectives

To reinforce skills in evaluating evidence

Teaching Ideas

USING THE WORKSHEET

The intent is to spend no more than 10–15 minutes on this lesson. It could also be assigned as homework, with students then discussing their answers in small groups, followed by the whole class quickly going over answers and discussing points of contention. If students suggest any criteria for evaluating evidence that are not on the class poster, have someone add them to the information on the poster.

EXTENDING THE ACTIVITY

As a follow-up, ask students to find and evaluate evidence in their textbook regarding the causes of the American Revolution.

Suggested Answers

1. The second story is more likely to be true because Philip should know that the teacher could check the story with his parents. Thus, the second story is able to be confirmed, whereas the first is not.

   The second story does, however, raise some questions: Why didn't you say anything about the wedding before the homework was due? Why didn't you do the homework earlier if you knew you were going to have to go to the wedding? Such questions would check the internal consistency of the evidence.

2. The Proclamation itself is more reliable, since it is a primary source. The book may, however, be a quicker—and more easily understood—source when the information is commonly known.

3. The letter from the British officer is more reliable because he is a primary source and has no reason to lie. Although he might exaggerate the amount of money he collected, he is unlikely to say he has done it unless he has.

   The colonial merchant of the second piece of evidence might accuse British officials of corruption with no real evidence—either because he wants to believe the story or because he wants to make the British look bad. Although the merchant may or may not be a primary source, one must be careful of this type of evidence because of a possible reason to lie.

4. Pontiac's evidence is more reliable. It tells us that, in the minds of the Indians, Amherst's policies were a key cause of the war. The key phrase here, however, is "in the minds of the Indians." There could have been other, more important causes for other groups of people. Also, this evidence doesn't show that Amherst's policies were "foolish," just that Pontiac considered them unfair to his people.

STRENGTHS

5. Mr. Temple is an expert on the topic and would understand what he was seeing.

He was in a position to learn the information.

Mr. Temple has no apparent reason to lie.

WEAKNESSES

• The source is secondary, although Mr. Temple may be a primary source. (It is not clear whether or not Temple saw Bernard's records. A summary of his statement is in a secondary source by Dickerson.)

There is no actual, physical evidence that Bernard collected money illegally. Temple's statements would be regarded as hearsay evidence in court.

Even if Governor Bernard had collected money through corruption, he may have been the only governor to do so. This would not justify the claim that "some governors" collected money from corruption.

WEAKNESSES

6. This information has no source. (End of analysis. Everyone in class should have recognized the lack of a source.)

Lesson 12: Identifying and Evaluating Comparison Arguments

Objectives

To recognize comparison reasoning

To evaluate comparison arguments

Teaching Ideas

USING THE WORKSHEET

The first section of the worksheet can be done quickly. It might be best to complete and discuss problem 6 before starting problem 7, which requires students to recognize comparisons in a longer, more sophisticated argument.

You might want to cue students that problem 7 is the same form of comparison as Problem 6; i.e., something got better or worse over time. Encourage them to refer back to problem 6 if they get stuck.

You might also want to discuss the first paragraph of the argument in Problem 7. Students should realize that this is not the author's argument but rather what other people have claimed. This form of argument (first telling the reader what others have said) is common in historical interpretations.

EXTENDING THE ACTIVITY

Students may want to know the information necessary to evaluating the comparison in Problem 7. A graph of all exports and imports for the years 1790–1820 (next page) might help students somewhat. For further research refer students to *Historical Statistics of the United States*.

Suggested Answers

1. This could be considered a comparison of before (running) to after (stopped), but this isn't central to the argument. The statement is mainly a cause-and-effect claim.

2. C

3. C

4. C

5. Nothing in the argument is being compared.

6. a. Case A: George's ability to play the piano last year

   Case B: His ability to play the piano this year

   b. It's a comparison of difference ("improved").

   c. It's difficult to think of differences or similarities that would weaken this conclusion. George is the same person. Even a different piano wouldn't account for such an improved level of playing.

d. Tunes seem like the most reasonable factor to compare. Other types of playing (i.e., chords, scales) could be cited, but by improving the playing of songs the person will most likely show improvement in other areas as well.

e. This is a strong comparison. [Unless the speaker doesn't know anything about music—or George got a player piano and didn't tell anyone!]

7. a. Compares American tobacco exports in 1770 to those in 1810.

b. It's a comparison of difference ("decrease").

c. The claim is that the end of the Navigation Acts accounts for the difference in American tobacco exports. Other possible factors could account for the difference, however, including a national shift to other exports; a general drop in economy between 1770 and 1810; trade restrictions on tobacco, either on the part of America (such as the Embargo Act) or of other countries; a war which might hinder trade; change in English demand for tobacco; changes in weather or growing conditions; growers leaving the market because of any number of reasons (low prices, soil depletion, lack of labor to harvest tobacco, increase in profitability of other products, etc.).

d. "Why were these dates picked?" is a question that immediately arises. Maybe they represent the general trend in exports before and after the American Revolution, in which case the comparison is reasonable. However, if the tobacco exports fluctuate quite a bit then the comparison is weak—for example, suppose tobacco exports were 50 million in 1769 and 98 million in 1809?

e. Because other possible differences are not considered, this is a weak comparison.

GRAPH OF EXPORTS AND IMPORTS, UNITED STATES: 1790–1820

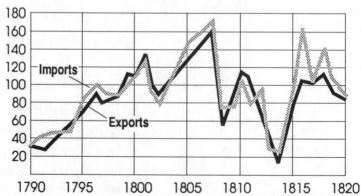

Lesson 13: Evaluating and Making Generalizations

Objectives

To evaluate given generalizations
To recognize reasonable generalizations
To make reasonable generalizations

Teaching Ideas

PREPARATION

Before students begin this worksheet, ask them to define a generalization and to explain how they might evaluate one. You may want to have them read or review the section on **Generalizations** in the "Guide to Critical Thinking" or the introductory worksheet (Worksheet H) on this type of reasoning.

USING THE WORKSHEET

Problems 1–4, like the introductory worksheet, focus on evaluating given generalizations. Students may wish to draw circle diagrams as they evaluate the problems. Since the sample in problem 4 is unclear, students are given a hint. (The sample is those who can run the government: free, adult, white, male landowners.)

Problem 5 gives the students choices for extending the information; problem 6 does not and thus may be difficult for some students.

EVALUATION

Remember that there is no single correct answer; focus more on the reasons for students' choices.

Suggested Answers

1. a. The generalization is that colonists hated the Tea Act. (It could mean all or most colonists.)

    b. Subgroups might include people with differing wealth, education, loyalty to England, occupations, locations, ages, and backgrounds. In other words, all people who lived in America.

    c. The sample is of colonists in four cities: Boston, New York, Philadelphia, and Charleston.

    d. No; the sample does not include people who lived inland, those who were not residents of larger towns, or those in the four mentioned cities who did not participate in the boycott.

    e. The generalization is weak because of those excluded from the sample [see 1 d, above].

2. a. The generalization is that most colonists were opposed to the Stamp Act.

    b. Subgroups for this generalization are the same as for problem 1 [see 1 b, above].

    c. The sample is of representatives from nine of the thirteen colonies. (It might be of more if the other colonies carried out the boycott also, but we don't know that from the given information.)

    d. Representatives at the Stamp Act Congress were probably selected by free, adult, white, male land-owners who were opposed to the Stamp Act—since that's the whole idea of organizing an opposition group. The same is true for organizing a boycott. This fails to consider many subgroups included in the generalization.

    e. The generalization has some credibility, since it is based on a sample that is somewhat representative. It is not, however, representative in all ways [see 2 d, above].

3.   a. The generalization is that a majority of adult Americans were influenced by *Common Sense*.

    b. Subgroups are the same as in 1 b (above), but the age is limited to adults.

    c. This is a large sample, comprising 5% of the entire population and a much larger percentage of the adult population. The sale of a publication to this large a segment of the population is quite impressive.

    d. While the sample is large, it may represent only those who were already Patriots or who had something to gain by revolution. It almost certainly represents only those who were literate, although illiterate people could have been influenced by the talk of those who had read it.

    e. The generalization does not represent all the subgroups in the colonies. For example, slaves did not read it. On the other hand, the large number of copies sold indicates that many of the colonists probably heard the argument; in this atmosphere, the argument about separating from England must have been discussed everywhere.

    One question remains, however: Were people who heard the argument "influenced" by it, as suggested in the generalization?

4.   a. The generalization is that the American Revolution brought freedom and political equality for all Americans.

b. Subgroups include all people who have lived in America since the time of the Revolution.

c. Sample is free, white, landowning, adult males.

d. No; many Americans were not free (indentured servants, slaves), not white (Indians, Blacks), not landowning (sharecroppers, slaves, servants), not adults, and not male.

e. The generalization is weak in a subtle way. People who make the *assumption* that political equality is intended for men will not recognize the weakness of the generalization.

5. C is probably the most closely drawn generalization, although B may also be acceptable, depending on how much revolutions have changed since the eighteenth century. A is clearly wrong, since it generalizes to nonrevolutionary situations.

6. Generalizing to other revolutionary situations might be reasonable, but changes—along with a host of other technological factors—would affect the outcome.

Lesson 14: Identifying Unstated Assumptions

Objectives

To identify and state hidden assumptions in written material

Teaching Ideas

PREPARATION

This skill may be introduced by either working through the introductory worksheets on assumptions (Worksheets I and J) or by asking questions about assumptions in some of the longer problems, such as Lessons 7, 10, or 15. When students see why recognizing unstated assumptions is important, they may be more interested in practicing the skill. (See the teacher's guides for Worksheets I and J for further suggestions.)

USING THE WORKSHEET

It is probably a good idea to keep the discussion of this worksheet short—maybe ten minutes or less.

EXTENDING THE ACTIVITY

Encourage students to identify assumptions that appear in their class discussions, also.

Suggested Answers

1. The public library will be open tonight and I can get there; it has sources on the Stamp Act; if I can't find any sources in the school library, they must not have any.

2. When Phil is not in this building, he is at home.

3. Colonists will not be fair, i.e., they will not convict fellow colonists; Colonists will not apply British law to their fellow colonists; British judges will be more fair in their verdicts than will colonists; the accused colonists are guilty (notice that the argument says "smugglers," not "accused smugglers").

4. "Bloody Massacre" implies the assumptions that lots of colonists were killed; the British killed them deliberately and for no good reason; the colonists involved had done nothing to the soldiers to deserve such treatment.

5. British and colonists are the only two groups with legitimate claim to the land (what about the Indians?); the colonists settled the land first (again, what about the Indians?); anyone who settles a place has legitimate claim to it.

6. People attribute more leadership qualities to large, tall, rugged-looking men. (Where does that leave women and small, short, refined-looking men?)

Lesson 15: What Caused the American Revolution?

Objectives

To evaluate evidence
To assess cause-and-effect reasoning
To recognize unstated assumptions
To evaluate generalizations

Teaching Ideas
PREPARATION

One fruitful way to start the lesson is to ask students to brainstorm causes for a revolution. After listing their ideas on the chalkboard, remind them of categories (social, political, economic, intellectual, religious, technological, biographical) that historians use to analyze events. Can they think of more possible causes?

Ask the students to shift their focus to the American Revolution.

- Do they have any information which would support or contradict any of their suggestions as causes for the American Revolution?
- What evidence would be needed to show that one cause is more likely than another?

You might also ask students what they think is the primary motivation of humans? (Economics? Ideas? Religion? Political rights? Power?) Such discussions will provide a broader perspective within which to place the three interpretations and help them identify the assumptions that each historian (or at least Historians B and C) in this lesson makes about human motivation.

APPROACHES TO
THE LESSON

Students may:
— read and evaluate each interpretation individually.
— read all three interpretations in one assignment, decide which they think is strongest, and explain why.
— choose one of the three points of view and defend it in a debate.

Any of these approaches would lend itself to research on questions raised about the causes of the Revolution.

USING A WORKSHEET

For students who need more structure for their analysis, use Worksheet L ("Analyzing Historical Interpretations"). Since the worksheet is fairly detailed (it hits all of the major skills), you may want to have students fill in only selected parts of it.

ADAPTING THE LESSON

Interpretations in this lesson are fairly sophisticated—although much less so than the original sources. One way to make the lesson less difficult is to have students read only Historians A and B. (Historian C's interpretation involves an understanding of a number of economic concepts.)

You might explain selected terms or vocabulary that some students might have difficulty understanding, such as *colony, empire, enlightenment, conspiracy, admiralty courts, Parliament, pamphlet, propaganda, currency, monopoly, pounds (£), capitalist, bankruptcy,* and *repealed*. You might also cue students that the words "England" and "Britain" are used interchangeably, as are "colonies" and "America."

DISCUSSING
THE INTERPRETATIONS

One way to guide a class discussion is to ask questions that focus students' attention on particular aspects of the interpretations. For example:

- What does each historian think motivates people?

- The date given after each historian is the date of publication. Why is that included? How might the date of writing influence what a historian says?

- To what extent did the French and Indian War change the equilibrium between the colonies and England?

- What was the main reason why the Proclamation of 1763 was passed? (Look at all three interpretations.)

- Were British laws intended primarily to pay off the debt from the French and Indian War or to protect British capitalists?

- Were colonists concerned primarily with the political or economic threat from England? Or did they feel they no longer needed England?

- How strong is the evidence used by the historians to support their arguments? How do they cite their evidence or sources?

- Why do the historians select the examples they do and leave out others? Make a chart of the British acts and actions explained by each historian. For example, why does Historian A emphasize the Proclamation of 1763, Historian B the Declaratory Act and troops, and Historian C the Navigation Acts?

Suggested Analyses

Historian A

MAIN IDEA

The Great War for the Empire was the main cause of the American Revolution.

KEY POINTS
AND EVIDENCE

Although Historian A presents some factual information, only one source is cited (Paragraph 6). Thus, the evidence is weak.

CAUSAL
REASONING

One cause-and-effect argument is that the French and Indian War led to large debts, which led to tax laws to raise revenue to pay off the debt, which led to protests, which led to Revolution. This all sounds logical, and there seems to be a reasonable connection between the causes and the effects. However, the statement in paragraph 5 that protests were "no more defiant" than others before this time undermines this cause-and-effect sequence.

Another cause-and-effect argument is that the French and Indian War removed the French as a threat, which led the colonists to think they didn't need England's support anymore (especially since England was so debt ridden), which led to Revolution. Students should ask if there is a logical connection between not needing another country's protection and trouble or revolution? Countries which no longer need each other often, but not always, split apart. Although this may have been an important cause, it does not seem to be sufficient to cause the Revolution.

OTHER
ASPECTS

The argument on the Proclamation of 1763 (paragraph 4) seems persuasive. The war led England to a need for Indian allies, which led to a promise of land to the Indians, which led to the Proclamation of 1763. Two questions need to be answered, however: Did the British break other promises they made to Indians? Could there have been other reasons for passing the Proclamation?

Historian B

MAIN IDEA

The main cause of the American Revolution was colonial beliefs that the British were threatening their freedom.

KEY POINTS
AND EVIDENCE

It seems reasonable that the frontier would cause people to believe in a simple life with local government (paragraph 3). Still, some evidence that people actually felt that way would be much more convincing.

CAUSAL
REASONING

One of the big questions raised about this interpretation is how many colonists believed this ideology? The author argues that the pamphlets were widely read which certainly strengthens his generalization that many colonists believed these things. (See **Generalizations** in the "Guide to Critical Thinking.") Nevertheless, on some points it is not clear how many colonists held these beliefs. One letter and one public statement are cited (endnote 6) to show the colonists believed the British troops were there to terrify them. No evidence is given to support the claim that the colonists felt the Declaratory Act gave them a choice between slavery and freedom (paragraph 6). To the contrary, some historians claim that the colonists, in their celebration over the repeal of the Stamp Act, virtually ignored the Declaratory Act.

Even if most colonists did believe that the British were threatening their political freedom, that does not mean that this belief was the main motivation for their action. Maybe most colonists were motivated mainly by economic discontent, for example, even though they also believed that the British threatened their political rights.

Note that Historian B cited evidence in endnotes, whereas the others cited sources within the text. Also, the 1960s was a period of political protest in the United States, which may have influenced this historian in writing his interpretation. This author seems to assume that beliefs (ideology) are a prime motivator of humans.

Historian C

MAIN IDEA

England's economic policies, which protected British capitalists at America's expense, were the main cause of the American Revolution.

KEY POINTS AND EVIDENCE

There is a fair amount of factual information given in the interpretation, such as specific numbers and laws. However, as with Historian A, there are not many sources cited. Without evidence, how do we really know that the Hudson Bay Company was a key to passage of the Proclamation of 1763 (paragraph 8) or that British sugar plantations were poorly run (paragraph 6)?

Both sources cited are from colonists (Dickinsen, paragraph 4; a Mechanic, paragraph 10), so they are primary sources. Both, however, have a reason to exaggerate the problems caused by the British.

CAUSAL REASONING

How do we know the colonists were actually hurt by the trade restrictions? It is possible that most colonists worked around the laws. If that's the case, then this interpretation loses much of its force.

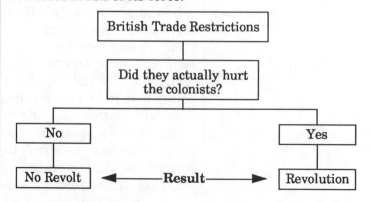

While it seems reasonable that most of the British laws cited here were probably passed to benefit British capitalists, there may have been other reasons for passing the laws as well. For example, as Historian A argues, maybe the Proclamation of 1763 had more to do with Indian policy than with the Hudson Bay Company.

British policy may not have been the only—or even the main—cause of the depression referred to in paragraph 11. Depressions are complicated phenomena which frequently have a number of causes. If British laws and actions were not the main causes then this interpretation is considerably weakened. Without the depression argument, Historian C only shows why rich American capitalists were upset with England. Rich people alone do not cause revolutions.

If the other economic classes revolted against England for some reason other than British mercantile policy, then it is not accurate to say that British mercantile policy is the main cause of the revolution.

Historian C devotes the first ten paragraphs to detailing British economic policies that drove American capitalists to revolution. Only paragraph 11 provides a reason for the vast majority of colonists to revolt. If British economic policy did not cause discontent among America's lower classes, then it is hard to see how British economic policy was the main cause of the Revolution.

This was written during the Great Depression, so the economic emphasis may have been a result of this perspective.

The author's frequent use of the word "capitalist" and emphasis on economics may indicate a Marxist orientation toward history. Historian C seems to assume that economic considerations are the primary motivations for humans.

Lesson 16: Was the Stamp Act Justified...?

Objectives

To evaluate evidence
To identify values and value judgments

Teaching Ideas

PREPARATION

The material in the student book consists entirely of sources to be used for a debate on the Stamp Act. The debate may be between two small groups (3 against 3) or a whole-class discussion and debate.

PROCEDURE

Tell students that the topic for their debate is the title of the lesson: Was the Stamp Act justified or were the colonists justified in not paying it? Ask each student to read through the documents, decide what he or she thinks, then write four or more arguments that support this position on the Stamp Act. Group students according to their stand on the debate topic, then have each group complie a common list of arguments. When they have completed their list, start the debate.

USING FOCUS QUESTIONS

Use focus questions such as those below to guide the debate when it wanders or flags.

- Do the colonists owe the British for settling in America, or did they do it basically on their own?
- Was the French and Indian War fought primarily to defend the colonists or help the British Empire?
- Is the Stamp Act fair? Were there precedents for it?
- Should the colonists have to pay taxes for the Empire? For troops?
- Why did Grenville grant a one-year delay?
- Were the colonies adequately represented in Parliament? Could they be?
- Were trials in Admiralty Courts right?
- Was the requirement for payment in hard money (specie) fair?
- Was the Stamp Act constitutional? Is that important?

EXTENDING THE ACTIVITY

As the students debate, write down some of their arguments. Reproduce these arguments for the next class—adding some questions about conclusions, evidence, cause and effect, and so forth—to focus students' attention on their own reasoning and evidence. (An example of such a worksheet and a chart summarizing the sources are included at the end of this lesson.)

ADAPTING THE ACTIVITY

You can make the lesson less difficult by having students omit sources 15–18, which deal with the more abstract concept of virtual representation.

You can shorten the lesson by having students read only certain sources (such as, 3, 6, 11, 15, 16, 18), by having each student read only a few sources, or by assigning a single source to each student for him or her to represent in the debate.

Suggested Analyses

Since any analysis will be of a classroom debate, no analysis could be written here. Watch for cause-and-effect reasoning, value claims, assumptions, evidence, and comparison reasoning (i.e., the colonists are in a different situation, so they can't be virtually represented) throughout the debate. Emphasize that students should request and evaluate evidence as the debate proceeds. Students should be asking, "What's your source for that claim?" then evaluating the source. Primary and secondary sources are mixed in this lesson, and the authors of the sources have a variety of frames of reference and ranges in objectivity (reason to lie).

SAMPLE TRANSCRIPTION OF DEBATE ARGUMENTS

(**B** = Supports British; **C** = Supports Colonists)

I.	**B**	Grenville gave the colonists a one-year delay before starting the tax to let them suggest alternatives.
II.	**C**	But he didn't agree with any of the colonial suggestions of an alternative to the tax.
III.	**B**	They were lousy suggestions. Why should he agree with them?
IV.	**C**	The Stamp Act is unconstitutional.
V.	**B**	But the colonies had already had stamp acts, and there were constitutions in the colonies.
VI.	**C**	The tax was unfair; the colonists shouldn't have had to pay it.
VII.	**B**	Yes, they should. The tax was used to pay the debt from the French and Indian War—a war fought by England to protect the colonies from the French.
VIII.	**C**	The War was fought for England, not the colonies. It started in Europe and happened to spread to the colonies.
IX.	**B**	That's what colonies are for—to help fight wars.
X.	**C**	Besides, the colonists, not the British, were the main ones who won the war.
XI.	**B**	You think the colonists won the war? You're a jerk.

SAMPLE QUESTIONS
ON DEBATE

1. What is the conclusion of argument I?
   (The tax was right; Grenville was fair.)
2. What is the conclusion of argument VII?
   (The tax was fair; Colonists should have to pay.)
3. What is a word which makes a value judgment in:
   a. Argument III? (lousy)
   b. Argument VI? (unfair)
   c. Argument VII? (should; protect)
4. Identify a value expressed in:
   a. Argument VII? (People should have to pay for wars that protect them.)
   b. Argument III? (People don't have to agree with lousy suggestions.)
5. What type of reasoning is used in:
   a. Argument V? (analogy/comparison)
   b. Argument IX? (sample/generalization)
6. How strong is the comparison in argument V?
   (False analogy; there is an important difference between the colonists taxing themselves (constitutional) and the British taxing the colonists (unconstitutional.)
7. What is the fallacy in argument XI?
   (Ad Hominem)

SUMMARY
OF SOURCES

Source No.	Supports	Topic Dealt With	Summary of Source
1	British	Precedent for the Stamp Act	NY and MA had stamp acts before, so it's okay now.
2	British	One-year delay	Delay so colonists could object or suggest alternatives.
3	Colonists	Grenville's response to Colonial representatives	• Grenville wouldn't give copies of the Act to colonial spokesmen. • Grenville said there should be no objections or alternatives. • Grenville said the tax was best for the colonies. • Objections wouldn't carry any weight in Parliament. • Colonists already had a Stamp Tax in NY.

Source No.	Supports	Topic Dealt With	Summary of Source
4	Colonists	One-year delay	Delay was to get colonists to agree with Stamp Act.
5	British	One-year delay	Colonists offered no real alternatives.
6	British	Who should pay?	Colonists should pay fair share for Empire and defense.
7	British	Who should pay?	Debt incurred for colonists, so colonies should help pay.
8	British	Small tax	Very small tax on the rich.
9	British	Why Colonists should pay	Colonies settled due to English care and protection.
10	Colonists	Why should Colonists pay?	Colonists owe nothing to England; they started and grew despite England; they can defend themselves.
11	Colonists	Representation	• No tax without representation. • Colonists can't be fairly represented in Parliament. • Admiralty Courts violate rights of trial by jury. • Colonists can't pay in specie.
12	Colonists	Representation	England would shift tax burden to unrepresented colonists.
13	Colonists	Representation	England would shift tax burden to colonists to pay for extravagent spending.
14	British	Small tax	Such a small tax is not a burden.
15	British	Virtual Representation	Some British towns have no actual representation but pay taxes, why shouldn't colonists?

Source No.	Supports	Topic Dealt With	Summary of Source
16	British	Virtual Represen- tation	MPs represent all people, sometimes at the expense of those in their own districts.
17	British	Virtual Represen- tation	General belief in England was that MPs should represent all the people in general.
18	Colonists	Virtual Represen- tation	• Colonists not virtually represented in British Parliament in the same way British nonvoters were. Actually, all British land was represented; no Colonial land was. • British could shift tax burden to colonists.

Lesson 17: Who Fired First at Lexington Green?

Objective

To evaluate evidence about a specific historical event

Teaching Ideas

USING THE WORKSHEET

This lesson asks students to chart information to evaluate evidence or sources of information. Ask the students to read through the evidence and complete the worksheet, paying particular attention to the strengths and weaknesses of the evidence according to the **PROP** questions. The last part of the assignment asks them to defend their decision on "Who fired first?" by writing a paragraph.

When the students have completed the assignment, have them discuss their answers in groups of three or four. Each group should agree on its answer of who fired first. As the class discusses the overall answer, many of the strengths and weaknesses of individual pieces of evidence should emerge. You can then decide whether to point out strengths and weaknesses that students do not mention.

ADAPTING THE LESSON

The lesson can be shortened by having the students read and evaluate only the first four pieces of evidence. You might also want to go over some of the difficult vocabulary with students before they read the evidence: *sworn deposition, testimony, militia, regulars, troops, instant, rod* (5 1/2 yards), *brandish, volley, Justice of the Peace, atrocity,* and *patriots.*

Suggested Analysis

1. **Parker (Colonist)**; "British fired first."

STRENGTHS

Primary source; was in a good position to see the event; swore to his testimony, (which was a serious thing in the 18th century).

WEAKNESSES

Reason to lie (doesn't want people to think his men started it); was probably nervous (which might affect what he thought he saw); probably expected British to fire first (which would influence his perceptions).

2. **Barker (British)**; "Colonists fired first."

STRENGTHS

Primary source; good position to see the event; personal diary (probably not trying to influence anyone); reported the same day as the event.

WEAKNESSES

Some possible reason to lie (but not a big factor in a diary unless he thought someone would read the diary); probably nervous; probably expected Colonists to fire first.

3. Fessenden (Colonist); "British fired first."

STRENGTHS

Primary source; sworn testimony; reported soon after the event (although he may have forgotten some important details in four days).

WEAKNESSES

Reason to lie; probably nervous; may not have been in good location to see who fired first (no mention made of where he was in relation to either group of soldiers).

4. Pitcairn (British); "Colonists fired first."

STRENGTHS

Primary source; good location; professional soldier (should know what was happening).

WEAKNESSES

Reason to lie (would not make himself look bad in a report to his commander); possibly nervous; expected the other side to start trouble.

5. Nathaniel Mullekin and 33 others (Colonist); "British fired first."

STRENGTHS

Primary source; given shortly after the event (although six days may have allowed them to "get their stories straight"); good location; sworn testimony; other people (thirty-four of them) say the same thing.

WEAKNESSES

Reason to lie; all 34 men saying the same thing isn't such a strength (one person probably wrote it out and the others agreed to it; how likely is it that all 34 saw exactly the same thing, as stated in this testimony?); sounds more like a justification than an objective description.

6. Steinberg (Historian); "British fired first."

STRENGTHS

Professional historians are supposed to have skills necessary to decide what really happened.

WEAKNESSES

Secondary source; use of emotional words (*embattled farmers, patriots, atrocity*) makes him seem biased toward the Colonists; no sources of his information given.

7. Wood (Colonists); "British fired first."

STRENGTHS

Primary source; good location.

WEAKNESSES

Reason to lie; testimony given more than 50 years after the event (memory fades and changes in that length of time).

8. Bateman (British); "British fired first."

STRENGTHS

Primary source; good location.

WEAKNESSES

Reason to lie (as prisoner he may think he will be harmed if he says the colonists fired first; very likely that he lied about the colonists not firing at all, as there were apparently several British wounded.

9. *London Gazette* (British); "Colonists fired first."

STRENGTHS

None

WEAKNESSES

Secondary source; nonobjective point of view, favorable to the British side.

Lesson 18: Analyzing Pictures as Arguments

Objectives

To evaluate visual evidence

To relate relevant information to hypotheses

Teaching Ideas

Have the students examine the pictures then consult the Relevant Information as they answer the questions. Students can discuss their answers in small groups or as a class. It might be preferable to give the students some of the information below regarding the artist and date of each painting, but there are advantages to having students make hypotheses on this first; i.e., it may encourage more careful observations; more hypotheses may be generated (although some may be incorrect); there is more of a "mystery," therefore a higher interest on the part of the students.

Rather than choosing a "most-accurate" depiction, it might be best just to ask the students give their hypotheses and discuss their reasons. The most accurate picture may be number 5, even though the technical quality may not be as good. The major points you may want to discuss are that Picture 2 appears inaccurate based on Relevant Information 2 and that picture 5 was done by someone who was at the scene a few weeks after the battle occurred.

Suggested Analyses of Pictures

PICTURE 1

It is probably pro-Colonist, since it shows the colonists as heroic and was painted from their side of the Green. It was actually painted by Henry Sandham in October 1886 for *Harper's Magazine*, but different hypotheses could reasonably be offered as to the date painted. (The **reasons** for students' drawing particular hypotheses are important, not the hypotheses themselves.) The painting accurately reflects the physical conditions (building location; light; tree leaves) but seems a little too dramatic, as indicated by the title, "The Dawn of Liberty." It shows colonists firing a volley at the British and point-blank at Pitcairn—inaccuracies that students might observe.

PICTURE 2

This picture is probably also pro-Colonist, since it shows them as heroic and was painted from their perspective. (It does, however, seem to show that the Colonists fired first, since the British troops look as if they still have their rifles on their shoulders.) It was painted sometime in the 1800s. Although the buildings are correctly located, the light seems about right, and the trees look right for mid-April, the painting appears inaccurate on several points: Relevant Information (RI) 2 says the British had few casualties, the colonists probably did not fire a volley at them; Pitcairn was not wounded—and the Colonists would not likely have missed him had they been as close as shown in the picture; no additional British troops are shown on the road from Boston to Lexington; a second line of British troops is shown to the right of the Meeting House.

PICTURE 3 | Since it was painted from the Colonists' perspective and shows the colonists as heroic, students may reasonable infer that the picture is pro-Colonist. In this painting by McNevin, students may especially note the dramatic scene of the woman (possibly Mrs. Harrington) holding the dead or wounded man. Several inaccuracies may be noted: the building on the left is facing the wrong direction; some of the shadows are wrong for sunrise; there appears to be the body of another woman on the steps of the building—and there were no women wounded or killed; the Green is shown larger than it actually was; the trees are too full for April in Massachusetts.

PICTURE 4 | This picture is pro-Colonists, since it is drawn from the colonist direction and shows the colonists in dramatic, heroic poses. Note that the British soldiers appear in outline, almost like ghosts, while the Colonists are filled in. There is no way to determine the accuracy of the drawing from the locations of buildings, since only one building is shown. The great majority of the colonists stood on the Green, however, not behind a stone wall—although there were apparently some Colonists behind a wall and several shots may have been fired from there. This drawing seeks to give a specific, and incorrect, impression of how the battle was fought.

PICTURE 5 | Although this was actually painted by a colonist, students might reasonably assume the artist was British, since the colonists are shown as retreating rather than as heroic. On the other hand, as with all the other pictures, the picture is from the direction of the colonists and seems to show that the British fired first. It was drawn by Ralph Earl, a colonist who was at Lexington a few weeks after the battle, and engraved by Amos Doolittle in 1775. The painting appears accurate in several respects: the shadows are about the right length for sunrise; the trees are about right for mid-April; the buildings look as if they are in the right locations. There are also, however, several inaccuracies: it shows British troops on all sides of the meeting house; no Colonial is firing, which they would have had to do if any British were shot.

Lesson 19: Effects of the American Revolution

Objectives

To develop and assess cause-and-effect reasoning
To recognize assumptions

Teaching Ideas
USING THE WORKSHEET

Ask the students to answer step 1 individually, then list their responses on the chalkboard. Answers will vary, but most students should be able to project three or four effects.

Step 2 asks students to focus on one of their projections and to consider criteria for deciding if a projected effect is reasonable. For example, if students suggest that one effect of the Revolution was a more democratic society, then they should consider what they would expect to see after the Revolution to confirm that hypothesis.

- Did Americans have more rights, such as freedom from search and trial by jury?
- Did they have more say in taxation policy?
- Did they have more control over government officials?

Students may be able to fill in the last two parts of this question without any research, but it is likely that they will have to gather some information from various sources.

Step 3 reminds students to consider categories when projecting effects. Cue them to consider effects that the Revolution had on individuals or on groups of people. Answers will vary, but students should be able to defend their choices.

Answers to step 4 may reveal that students considered only the effects on white males. Asking them to think about and respond to the following questions will make them more sensitive to a multicultural perspective of historical events.

- What were the effects on women, blacks, Indians, or other minorities?
- How did you arrive at a monocultural frame of reference for examining events?
- How does that frame of reference affect how you view the world?
- How did the various groups in America view the Revolution; what were their dreams, goals, and aspirations? Were their hopes met?
- From this perspective, how revolutionary was the American Revolution?
- Has the American Revolution continued since 1776?

EXTENDING ACTIVITY

Give students copies of the following letters exchanged by Abigail and John Adams. Ask for their reactions.

Sunday evening, March 31, 1776

Dear John,

I am so excited to hear that you will be helping to write the Declaration of Independence and the laws for our new nation. I hope that you will remember the ladies, and be more generous to them than your ancestors were to the women of their time. Do not give husbands so much power over wives. Remember, all men would be rulers of women if they could. If you continue to ignore us, we will refuse to obey any of your laws which we have never had any say about at all. Regard us as human beings, created equal like you.

Love,
Abigail

Wednesday evening, April 4, 1776

Dear Abigail,

As to the suggestions in your last letter, I cannot but laugh. Everywhere there are people refusing to obey the laws. Children are disobedient, schools and colleges are disturbed. Indians are fighting back, and the black have become disrespectful of their masters. But your letter was the first announcement that another tribe, much larger in number and power than all the rest, has grown unhappy with their condition. You have become so rude that I cannot ignore it. Believe me, we know better than to throw away our masculine systems. We refuse to give up our power to eventually be ruled by the petticoat [women].

Fondly,
John

UNIT 4
THE CONSTITUTION

LESSON 20: Evaluating a Constitution

Objectives

To identify values and value judgments
To recognize unstated assumptions
To relate relevant information to hypotheses

Teaching Ideas
PREPARATION

This lesson focuses on the weaknesses of the Articles of Confederation by giving students a summary of the Articles and asking them to infer the weaknesses.

ADAPTING THE LESSON

Make the lesson challenging by asking students to read the summary, answer the four questions below the summary, then share and defend their answers in a class discussion.

For more structure, have students read the summary and refer to it as they complete the worksheet on analyzing a constitution (student text, pages 92–93). To shorten the lesson, have students answer only selected items on the worksheet.

NOTE

Students should either complete and discuss the worksheet OR answer the questions at the end of the summary, since they are similar.

Suggested Answers
ANALYZING THE
GOVERNING CONSTITUTION

1. Powers granted to the central government include the right to pass laws, declare war, make peace, manage foreign relations, decide disputes between states (by appointing a committee), and borrow and set the value of money.

2. Many important powers are missing: the right to collect taxes; no executive branch (so no way to enforce laws); no power to control trade between states; no regular national courts to settle disputes; no power to raise an army; no power to enforce treaties.

3. a. What if it became obvious that the national government needed a new power? There may not necessarily be anything wrong with this reserve power, however. (Point out that this is what is in the Tenth Amendment of the present Constitution.)

   b. Large-population states wouldn't like that.

c. The delegates would be tightly controlled by the wishes of the state legislatures; one-year term may not be long enough to accomplish anything; possibility of having entirely new and inexperienced Congress every year.

d. The central government has no power to collect taxes itself.

e. Not many bills would pass; not much would be done by the government.

f. The constitution can't be changed to meet new circumstances; each state has power of total veto (in effect any one state can control the others by keeping from them something they want or need).

4. Sovereignty is divided, with the states having supreme power in some areas and the national government in others. Most of the power is with the states—a confederation form of government.

5. • Constitutions should be written.

• States' rights are supreme.

• Strong central governments are undesirable and unresponsive.

• Sovereignty can be shared between two levels of government.

• Too much change is bad.

• Defense is an important function of the national government.

• The national government has important economic functions.

6. • Colonial America emphasized local government, rather than a strong central government.

• The Revolution made Americans distrustful of strong central governments, such as the British government.

• Americans opposed British taxation of them. It seems natural that they would hesitate to give that power to another central government.

• Americans disliked governors, so it makes sense they would avoid executive power and instead give the power to a legislature.

• What about attitudes toward judiciary? Toward debt? Toward elitism?

U. S. GOVERNMENT,
1791–1797

Overall, this government will not be very effective because it lacks key powers.

- The government will be unable to make Americans pay their debts to England so England will be unlikely to cooperate with America. (A, B)

- The new government will be unable to raise enough money to send or support an army in the West to fight the British, Spanish or Indians. We'll get no respect from foreigners. (B, C, D)

- Since the central government has no means of raising—or forcing the states to raise—money, it will be unable to pay the debt. (E)

- Interstate trade will suffer from different state money (F) and interstate tariffs. (G)

- Because it would means interfering with the rights of states and individuals, the government will not prevent the bankrupting of American businesses due to the flooding of the American market by British goods. (H)

- Although exports may go down initially (I), they may actually increase as trade improves with areas outside the British Empire.

- The question of land claims by various states was a real problem area, but the Articles handled it well in the land ordinances.

Lesson 21: Shays's Rebellion

Objectives

To assess cause-and-effect reasoning
To relate relevant information to hypotheses

Teaching Ideas
USING THE WORKSHEETS

Ask the students to read and answer the questions on Historian A's viewpoint, then discuss their answers as a class. Have them read Historian B's view, answer the questions, and discuss their answers. For each historian, ask students if the argument shows that Shays's Rebellion was an important cause of the Constitution?

When students have discussed the two interpretations, ask them to read the Relevant Information on pages 97–98 in their text and answer the questions. Have students discuss their answers in small groups then as a class.

GUIDING
CLASS DISCUSSION

You might want to focus this discussion by helping students distinguish the concepts of "necessary and sufficient cause." The Relevant Information seems to indicate that Shays's Rebellion was neither "necessary" (the Constitution would have been written without it) nor "sufficient" (the Rebellion by itself would not have brought about the Constitution) to the writing of the Constitution.

Press students to analyze and defend their own cause-and-effect arguments. As hypotheses are proposed, ask what the connection is between the cause and the effect.

Suggested Answers
HISTORIAN A

1. Cause: Shays's Rebellion; Effect: Constitution written to strengthen the central government

2. Students will offer differing opinions, but someone should suggest that Historian A makes no connection between the Rebellion and the delegates to the Constitution. Is there evidence that the delegates talked about the Rebellion? Did the Rebellion show that the government under the Articles of Confederation was weak? Did people think Massachusetts needed help from the central government to handle the Rebellion? Were there other possible reasons for wanting a strong central government?

3. The argument is an example of *post hoc, ergo propter hoc* (after this, therefore because of this) reasoning. It argues that since the delegates passed a stronger central government right after Shays's Rebellion, they passed it because of Shays's Rebellion. The argument is therefore weak, since it

doesn't show **how** Shays's Rebellion led to a stronger central government—it only assumes that it did so.

4. Historian B argues that the delegates to the Constitutional Convention were men of property who were afraid of revolt. Thus, Shays's Rebellion motivated them to create a stronger central government, i.e., the Constitution. As an additional connection, Historian B offers the quotation by Washington, indicating that the Rebellion was indicative of rising anarchy.

5. Historian B's argument is clearly stronger than Historian A's, but, as we shall see, the connection is not as strong as it might appear.

6. Students will offer differing opinions on this question. Some will argue that the information shows little connection between Shays's Rebellion and the writing of the Constitution and cite the following information:

   • Many delegates were convinced of the need for a strong central government before Shays's Rebellion (A, B, H).

   • Other factors may have been as (or more) important as causes (D, E).

   • The Rebellion was not an important focus in the debate at the convention (F).

   • The Rebellion could have been used to argue either for or against the Constitution (G).

   • There is no correlation between support of the Rebellion and opposition to the Constitution (J).

   • The state most affected by the Rebellion (Massachusetts) voted against the Constitution (I).

   Others may argue that some information tends to show that there may have been a connection between Shays's Rebellion and the writing of the Constitution.

   • Congress may have been pushed to vote for the Constitutional Convention because of Shays's Rebellion, since it voted right after the height of the insurrection (M, N).

   [By now students should have learned that this is the *post hoc* (after, therefore because of) fallacy. We need to see evidence that the representatives voted for the Convention because of Shays' Rebellion.]

- Delegates may have favored the Constitution due to increased public opinion pressure stemming from the *Anarchiad* articles (L).

  [Again, students should be able to see that the connections (from the newspaper articles to the public to the delegates) are not made. We really don't **know** if the *Anarchiad* articles influenced the writing of the Constitution.

7. Other possible causes are shown in Relevant Information D, E, and H.

8. Students will disagree with each other, but the Relevant Information suggests that it probably would have been written in substantially the same way due to other perceived weaknesses in the Articles of Confederation.

9. The information suggests that it was not an important cause. Other questions will raise further problems with the Rebellion as an important cause; for example:

- How was a strong central government supposed to prevent or subdue such insurrections?

  Some evidence suggests that the Rebellion was caused by the internal politics of Massachusetts and that Massachusetts was able to put down the Rebellion without much difficulty.

Lesson 22: Evaluating Sources

Objectives

To identify and evaluate evidence

Teaching Ideas
USING THE WORKSHEET

Have students fill in the worksheet and discuss their answers as a group. Although students may focus on the four main criteria (PROP) for evaluating the evidence in problems 8–10, other criteria should arise as well. After discussing answers to these problems, ask students how they could check further on these pieces of evidence.

Suggested Answers

1. E; the mother is the source.

2. I; gives specific heights, but no source for the heights.

3. I

4. E

5. N

6. I; what follows "for example" is information, but no source is given.

7. E; Hamilton and Randolph are sources, but they don't tell us where the author of this argument got the information, so they aren't as strong as having more specific sources.

Strengths

8. • He's a primary source, if the other students told him their real motives.

Weaknesses

   • It's more likely that Bob is a secondary source and is only guessing why the other students don't like him.

   • Bob has an obvious reason to lie to remove blame from himself for his unpopularity. Actually, his statement indicates a likely cause—arrogance.

   • There are no other sources supporting Bob's claim, and it's a public statement.

Strengths

9. • Primary source. King undoubtedly observed the Antifederalists and heard them present their objections to the Constitution. On the other hand, it is doubtful that the Antifederalists actually stated their distrust of the rich and educated, so King probably inferred, rather than directly observed, this motive.

   • Private source. King is less likely to lie in a private letter to someone on the same side of an issue than he is to someone on the other side.

Weaknesses

- While King may not have had a direct reason to lie in a private letter, his own frame of reference may have caused him to distort what he saw.

- His letter summarizes the motives of his opponents. How often do we do this fairly?

- Notice that he says the objections are not to the Constitution itself, thus minimizing the objections.

- There is no other evidence supporting King's claims. Some statements by Antifederalists would help decide the accuracy of King's evidence.

Strengths   10.

- There are a number of historians who agree on the claim.

- These are reputable historians, so they have the weight of authority on their side. They are scholars who are supposed to research carefully.

- Historians have little reason to lie about a subject like this.

Weaknesses

- It's a secondary source.

- While all the authors apparently agreed, having separate sources agree (independent verification) is more desirable.

- Although the authors have little reason to lie, their frames of reference may lead them to distort how they interpret what they have found.

Lesson 23: Arguments over Constitutional Ratification

Objectives

To evaluate methods of eliminating alternatives
To assess cause-and-effect reasoning
To evaluate comparisons
To identify unstated assumptions

Teaching Ideas

USING THE ARGUMENTS

The two summarized arguments can be used in several different ways.

- Have students evaluate the arguments on their own then discuss their evaluations.
- Use the more structured analysis questions provided on the worksheet to stimulate and structure a class discussion.
- Have a debate between Mr. Madison (Argument A) and Mr. Yates (Argument B).
- Have small-group analyses of the two positions.

MODIFYING THE LESSON

These arguments may prove too abstract and difficult for some students. Make them more concrete by asking:

- Do all groups in our society have the same interests?
- Auto companies want a tariff on foreign cars, while consumers want the best car at the lowest price. What other groups have conflicting interests?

  (Farmers want government aid to keep prices high; taxpayers may not want to pay for such aid. One religion wants government tax help; people of other religions wouldn't want to pay taxes for that purpose. Oil companies want to drill for oil in the ocean; environmentalists want to prevent drilling.)

- A group with a particular interest (like "farmers") is called a faction. Ideally, people will decide their attitude toward issues based on the public good (what's good for the whole nation), not on their own personal interest. Are factions likely to base their decisions on the public good?
- How can a country control factions and promote government policy based on the public good?

A second (and more structured) approach to the concepts of "faction" and "the public good" is provided by the **"Worksheet on Making Government Policy."** Students may answer the questions individually then discuss as a class the reasons for their opinions.

EXTENDING THE LESSON

Several interesting issues can arise from these readings.

- Should citizens know their representatives well?
- What role should citizens play in democratic society?

- How have changes in communications (especially media) affected factions?
- What role does "trust" play in government?

Any of these, and many others, could be the subject of student essays.

Suggested Answers
ANALYZING THE
RATIFICATION ARGUMENTS
Argument A

1. The main point is that the Constitution is a very good framework for government since it forms a large republic to control factions.

2. Madison says that factions are caused by people with different opinions exercising their liberty to form groups that promote their own interests. This seems like a reasonable argument, since there is a good connection between differing opinions and factions and since it is hard to think of any other causes for factions.

3. Madison also uses "eliminating alternatives." In fact the basic structure of the argument uses this type of reasoning. He says we can either control the causes or the effects of factions. Neither of the two options for controlling the causes is a good idea. Thus, the only viable option is to control the effects. The proposed method for controlling the effects is through competing factions in a large republic.

    In each case, students should question whether the two alternatives offered are really the only possibilities. Are there any other options for preventing factions or controlling their effects?

4. Some possible beliefs held by Madison about good government are:

    - Governments should make policy for the public good, not particular interests.

    - Governments should prevent any one faction from controlling the policy-making.

    - Liberty is important to good government.

5. Whether a large republic today will still be able to prevent factions from dominating the government is an analogy or comparison. Students should ask how today's situation is similar to and different from the situation in 1787.

    (It is similar in that people still combine into factions. It is different in that communication abilities have broken down the distance barrier in a large republic. Thus, today's factions would have less difficulty combining to enhance their own interests and it becomes more questionable whether a large republic would prevent factions from dominating government.)

Argument B

6. The main point is that the Constitution should be rejected because it will promote strife and factional thinking.

7. Under the new Constitution the central government will dominate the states and continuously expand its power at the expense of state power.

   The author cites Article 6 and Article 1, Section 8 to make his point, saying that these clauses could be used to justify passing almost any law. While it could be used this way (showing a danger to states rights), it might not. The clause is open to interpretation. In using this argument the author anticipates the great debates over the "elastic clause" (Article 1, Section 8) in cases such as *McCulloch V. Maryland*.

8. Two types of reasoning predominate. The first is proof by authority, which is why the author quotes from Montesquieu. Note the importance of the audience to this point. Among Americans in the 1780s, Montesquieu was a recognized authority on government. The second type is cause-and-effect reasoning, i.e., large republics fail because of their size. Students should ask if a large republic **necessarily** leads to these effects.

9. One type of reasoning is comparison. The Greek and Roman Republics didn't work when they became large, so the United States as a large republic won't work. Maybe there are important differences, however, between the ancient republics and the United States in the 1780s. Others might see a cause-and-effect argument, with the author arguing that the large size of the republics caused them to decline into tyrannical governments. Students should ask if there might be other causes for tyrannical governments. (It seems quite likely that there were other causes.)

10. Students will disagree in their assessment of paragraphs 6 and 7. Is it necessary for representatives to know the views of most of their constituents on

an issue for the public good to be protected? Must they know the views of all of their constituents or only those who express their views to the representative? Is there a way to gather views of large numbers of people? (What about polls?)

Questions could also be posed for paragraph 7. Do people necessarily have to know their representatives before they will support the laws? Does unfamiliarity breed suspicion?

11. Assumptions this author makes are:

- History is a good place to search for perspective on present-day problems.

- The written constitution is a key to power relationships in governments.

- Article 1, Section 8 will be interpreted loosely, thus expanding federal power.

- The audience can read and comprehend his arguments.

- The audience will recognize Montesquieu and Beccarari as illustrious authorities on government.

- A government becomes less efficient as the number of representatives increases.

- People generally suspect the motives of people they don't know personally.

Comparing the Arguments

12. A new, large republic is being established. The new government is based on representatives, not democracy.

13. (Opinion)

Lesson 24: An Argument On the Constitution

Objectives

To evaluate generalizations
To evaluate comparisons
To identify unstated assumptions

Teaching Ideas

This reading summarizes arguments made by James Madison in "The Federalist Papers," Numbers 18, 19, and 20.

ADAPTING THE LESSON

If students need more background to understand the reading, questions about confederacies, ancient Greece, ancient Rome, council, league, tyranny, Germany, Netherlands, Athens, Sparta, and Philip of Macedonia can be discussed in class. Detailed knowledge of these terms is not, however, necessary to understand the reasoning used in the argument.

As students read and evaluate the argument, you may wish to cue them to watch for the main type of reasoning.

Analysis Points

Main point

The new constitution should be adopted.

Reasoning

Basically, Madison uses generalization to make his argument. He selects four historical examples to show that confederacies have not worked, and concludes that therefore the United States confederacy won't work. In evaluating this argument, the key questions are:

• Are these four examples representative of confederacies as a whole?

• Does the general trend apply to the confederacy in the U. S.?

Some students may see the argument as a comparison of the four examples to the United States. Here, the key question becomes how the two cases are different. If there are important differences between the United States on the one hand and the four examples on the other hand, then the comparison is weakened.

Unstated assumptions

• The audience knows something about the chosen historical examples.

• People and states should work for the general good, not for their own particular interests.

Lesson 25: Writing, Ratifying the Constitution: Two Interpretations of Motive

Objectives

To identify the main idea and unstated assumptions in an argument

To evaluate generalizations and evidence

To assess cause-and-effect reasoning

To identify logical fallacies, specifically "Straw Man" and "Special Pleading"

Teaching Ideas

PREPARATION

Since the two interpretations in this lesson concern the motives of the Founding Fathers in writing and supporting ratification of the Constitution, they focus on causation.

It is important that students understand the differences between *real* property and *personal* property (see paragraph 3 and endnote 2, Historian A). Ask students to identify and give examples of each type of property and to explain how each would be affected by the new Constitution. They should also be able to explain why personal property holders might benefit from—and real property holders might be hurt by—the new Constitution.

USING THE ARGUMENTS

Since Historian B's entire argument is an attempt to refute Historian A, the recommended way of using these readings is to have students read and evaluate Historian A first. When they have discussed Historian A's viewpoint as a class, the students can read Historian B. This will help them see weaknesses in Historian A's argument that they might not see without much research.

Analysis Points

HISTORIAN A   *Main point*

The Constitution was an economic document written and pushed through, despite widespread opposition by the propertyless and small, debtor farmers, by a small group of men who understood and protected certain economic interests.

Assumptions

Students should notice several of these. (Paragraph numbers are referenced in parentheses.)

- Historian A assumes that James Madison's thinking in the Federalist Papers is representative of the thinking of the delegates in general (6). (Hasty generalization.)

- He assumes that the positive powers granted in the Constitution were solely or mainly to protect property. The power to wage war, however, has mainly a political, not economic, purpose. Other powers listed also have noneconomic purposes. (8).

(HISTORIAN A)

- He assumes Antifederalists took longer than Federalists to get organized (10).
- He assumes that Federalists controlled the scheduling of the ratifying conventions (10).
- He assumes that because the writers of the Constitution had an economic stake in it, they wrote it mainly to protect their interests (4, 5, 9).

Reasoning | Several types of reasoning are used in this argument.

Cause and Effect: Historian A argues (9) that the delegates had an economic stake in the Constitution and wrote it to make money. There is a reasonable connection between having an economic stake and doing something to gain or protect that stake, but it isn't an absolute result. Other possible motivations might include to help the country, to help their state, or to protect the country from losing unity. Historian A should show evidence that economics was the motive. (One lesson to be learned from this is that motive is very hard to prove.)

Generalization: Does Madison represent the thinking of all or most of the delegates (6)?

Do the parts of the Constitution cited by Historian A (paragraphs 6 and 7) fairly represent the whole Constitution or were only the economic clauses cited to make it look like an economic document? If only certain parts were pulled out, Historian A is using the fallacy of "special pleading." (See the "Guide to Critical Thinking.")

How large is the sample from which the author makes the generalization that supporters of the Constitution were mainly from coastal areas and opponents were mainly from farm regions (10)? What does "mainly" mean? What percentages were from each area?

Evidence | No evidence is given to support some important points; e.g., that a majority of people were opposed to the Constitution in a number of states (10). Also, no evidence points to the actual motives of the delegates to the Constitutional Convention. There is only the possibility that their ownership of certain assets influenced them to write the Constitution so as to increase or protect these assets.

Endnote 1 looks fine. The Treasury files are a primary source and, although the biographies are secondary sources, it seems that the information would be easily accessible to most people. It seems unlikely that either source has a reason to lie, but delegates may not have reported all their assets.

(HISTORIAN A)

Endnote 2 gives no source for its information.

Endnote 6, cited to confirm the important point that supporters of the Constitution were mainly from coastal areas and opponents mainly from farm areas (10), is a secondary source. Historian A should have done his own research on this key point.

Additional points

Although Historian A says (9), "...the idea of the Constitution as a piece of abstract legislation reflecting no economic interests is entirely false," it is hard to believe that many people view the Constitution quite that way. Most probably think it was mainly abstract legislation or was a result of practical politics and compromise. Historian A has used the "straw man" fallacy (putting words in other people's mouths; see the "Guide to Critical Thinking").

HISTORIAN B

Because Historian B's argument is an attempt to refute the points argued by Historian A, no formal analysis of Historian B's view will be made here. Rather, a few random points will be raised.

- Even though the interpretation contains only two endnotes, the evidence is much stronger than Historian A's. Both endnotes indicate that a great deal of research, mostly from primary sources, was done. Furthermore, the evidence supports two central points in the argument regarding the delegates and the ratifying conventions.

- Some points are not supported by evidence; for example, that most people were property owners (3) or small farmers (5), or that almost all men owned property (6).

- The conflicting interests of the delegates and the lack of correlation between votes on the Constitution and economic interests undermines a great deal of Historian A's argument.

- Historian B also commits the "straw man" fallacy when he says (3) "...if we assumed that property or personal gain was their only motive." Historian A says that the delegates had economic interests, but never quite says economics was their only motive. In fact, in endnote 3 he specifically denies that personal gain was the only motive.

Objectives

Lesson 26: Foreign Views of the Constitution

To identify values and value judgments

To recognize and evaluate generalizations

To recognize logical fallacies, specifically "Special Pleading"

Teaching Ideas

PREPARATION

This lesson consists of translated and summarized excerpts from Argentine (Country A) and Soviet Union (Country B) history textbooks. You may choose to have students read the viewpoints and answer the evaluation questions independently or in small groups before proceeding with class discussions.

Since the vocabulary may be difficult, you may want to discuss certain words before assigning the reading. Some definitions and explanations are given in parentheses.

Suggested Answers

1. Country A seems concerned with stable, long-lasting government ("it still governs" the U.S. today); wise, prudent leadership (Washington's "prudent action"); violence or violent opposition ("eliminating the violent opposition"); a constitutional government; division of powers; and independence.

2. The country in Viewpoint A is Argentina. Although this cannot be inferred from the reading, some students should note the reference to Latin American independence in the last sentence as a clue to a Latin American country.

3. Country B seems concerned with power of the executive; dominance of capitalists and slaveholders; the relationship of social classes; property (economics) controls on the right to vote; the situation of the "masses" (poor and minorities); reality of personal freedoms; and development of the economy.

4. The country in Viewpoint B is the Soviet Union. Emphasis on social class, economics, and the failures of the Constitution should be good clues to the country. Additionally, certain vocabulary ("bourgeoisie class," "capitalists," "masses," "revolutionary workers") might cue students that the country has a strong socialist influence.

5. This should provide an interesting discussion. The main lesson students should learn is that what is emphasized and what is left out is a key way of

determining a point of view, even an extremely slanted point of view. This is the fallacy of special pleading—emphasizing favorable information while ignoring unfavorable information. Watching for emphasis and omissions is one way of recognizing the author's frame of reference. Another cue is vocabulary with emotion-laden connotation or that is specific to a given economic or social outlook.

Lesson 27: Evaluating Hypothetical Constitutions

Objectives

To assess cause-and-effect reasoning
To relate relevant information to hypotheses

Teaching Ideas

This lesson focuses on the factors which cause some constitutions to succeed and others to fail. More specifically, it is intended to make students thoughtfully consider why the Constitution of the United States has been so successful. Some interpretations focus on the wisdom of the founding fathers and the document itself. This lesson should prod students to consider other factors as well.

PREPARATION

Begin the lesson by asking students if they think the United States Constitution has been successful. What do they mean by "success"? How would they measure the success of a constitution? (Possible answers: It lasts a long time; the government is stable under it; people obey its rules; it remains as the supreme law of the land; it protects individual rights.) Students' answers will likely contain assumptions and value judgments that can also be examined.

USING THE SUMMARIES

Have the students read the descriptions of Countries A–F, write their hypotheses about the probability for the success of each constitution, then discuss their answers in small groups. Remind them that they are basically answering one question: "How long do you think the constitution of each country will last as an effective frame of government?"

After students have discussed their hypotheses, ask them to identify factors that cause the success or failure of constitutions (see p. 128). Students can recognize these factors by looking at the reasons for their answers.

USING THE WORKSHEETS

The first worksheet helps students analyze factors. It extends the lesson by asking them to identify the most and least important factors, giving a ten-year update on the countries, asking them to react to claims about constitutions, and posing questions about constitutions and rights today.

The second worksheet describes a real country, the Philippines. You could use this instead of or in addition to the hypothetical descriptions in the student book. This worksheet could also be used to extend the lesson from discussion of what makes constitutions successful to what makes democracies successful.

Suggested Answers

Answers will vary considerably. The following chart provides an overview of possible factors, including evaluations of the constitutions of the six countries. On the chart, "No" indicates a negative factor; "Yes" indicates a positive factor; "?" indicates that the impact of the factor is unclear; "—" indicates that the factor is not considered in the country's description.

FACTORS	*A*	*B*	*C*	*D*	*E*	*F*
1. *Does it have democracy now?*	No	Yes	Yes	No	Yes	No
2. *Was it ratified by the average people or their representatives?*	No	Yes	Yes	Yes	No	No
3. *Does it show the limits of government?*	No	—	No	Yes	No	Yes
4. *Does it protect specific rights?*	No	Yes	Yes	Yes	No	Yes
5. *Is it difficult, but not impossible, to amend?*	—	No	No	Yes	No	Yes
6. *Are the people in favor of the constitution?*	No	Yes	Yes	Yes	?	?
7. *Do the people have a tradition of participation in democratic government?*	No	No	No	?	Yes	No
8. *Is there a large middle class?*	Yes	No	No	No	Yes	Yes
9. *Do most people own their own land and property?*	Yes	—	No	No	Yes	No
10. *Has there been an absence of violence, especially between social classes?*	No	No	?	No	Yes	No
11. *Do most people share the same basic values?*	No	No	?	No	Yes	?
12. *Do most people share the same culture and language?*	—	No	—	No	Yes	?
13. *Are most people literate?*	—	No	—	No	Yes	Yes
14. *Is their country's region peaceful (no threats from neighboring countries)?*	—	Yes	—	—	—	No
15. *Is there a stable economy?*	—	—	—	No	Yes	Yes
16. *Does the new government have good leaders?*	No	—	—	—	Yes	No
17. *Is the government respected?*	No	?	?	No	Yes	No
18. *Is there trust in the government and its leaders?*	No	Yes	—	No	Yes	No
19. *Is it a capitalist (private business) economy?*	—	—	Yes	Yes	Yes	No
20. *Are the people patriotic? Do they give allegience to the country?*	—	No	Yes	—	—	—
21. *Was the constitution written by representatives of the people?*	No	Yes	No	No	No	—
22. *Were the writers of the constitution practical people?*	—	—	Yes	No	—	—
23. *Do most people think the new constitution is needed?*	—	—	—	—	Yes	—

Lesson 28: Evaluating Arguments About the Constitution

Objectives

To evaluate comparisons and generalizations
To recognize unstated assumptions

Teaching Strategies

Have the students fill in their answers, compare them in small groups, and discuss them as a class.

EXTENDING THE LESSON

Ask students to review their decisions. Are they consistent? Do their later decisions follow the precedents set in earlier decisions? If not, why were precedents overturned? Do their decisions make it clear when free speech is and is not protected? Ask the students to identify each incident and place it in one of the following categories— "Free Speech is Protected When..." or "Free Speech is **Not** Protected When... ."

Suggested Answers

1. Students should recognize this as a generalization (sample) problem in which the sample represents twelve of thirteen states and a large number of voters.

   On the other hand, Indians, blacks, women and other groups were excluded from the sample. Did this Constitution govern them, also? Property qualifications in some states further restrict the sample. The percentage of people who actually voted would help us better assess the sample. Some historians argue that a majority of the people opposed the Constitution and were underrepresented at the state ratifying conventions.

2. All drawbacks of the first sample apply here, and this sample is even more restricted. To what extent delegates actually represent their districts is an important issue, since the sample is of only 55 people.

3. Students should recognize the comparison of propertyless men to women. Are there important differences in terms of voting? They should also recognize the assumption that wives will vote the way their husbands vote. Third, they should notice that the author equates wives with women. What about single women? This argument has no weight against their voting.

4. If students say no one should be restricted from voting, ask them to consider the following groups: young children, criminals, insane people, aliens (residents who are not citizens of the country), people who know little about our government or history. Tell the class that the Constitution leaves voting qualifications for the states to determine.

Lesson 29: Constitutional Conflict: The Bill of Rights and Free Speech

Objectives

To evaluate comparison reasoning
To identify values and value judgments

Teaching Ideas

PREPARATION

This lesson focuses on the idea of the living Constitution, one which evolves based on interpretations by the Supreme Court. It is meant only as an example, for many other rights could also have been made into lessons by selecting a series of Supreme Court cases on a particular right. Moreover, many other cases could be selected to expand on the right considered in this lesson: free speech.

GUIDING THE DISCUSSION

The cases inherently involve reasoning by comparison. When students give their decisions, ask why they decided the same as or different from previous cases. This question will force students to think about how the previous cases were similar to or different from the case under discussion. Students will also become involved with value clarification as they explain why, in a particular case, they think speech should be restricted.

USING THE CASES

There are several possible approaches to this lesson. One is to have the students write their decisions to all the cases, discuss their decisions in small groups, then present and defend each decision to the class.

A second strategy is to have the students decide on all the cases and then discuss the first case. When the discussion ends, tell the students what the court actually decided, then have them review the second case to see if they would alter their decision. This strategy, which gives more weight to precedent, can be followed with each case.

EXTENDING THE LESSON

You might want to discuss with the class the relationship of the Supreme Court to state and local law and the application of the federal Constitution, through the Fourteenth Amendment, to state and local government.

Case Decisions

Since student decisions and rationale will vary considerably, only the actual Supreme Court decision is given for each case.

Schenck

The court ruled unanimously to uphold Schenck's conviction. Justice Holmes wrote that in peacetime the leaflets would have been protected by the First Amendment, but during a war they were not. The circumstances are a factor in deciding the limits of free speech. The question is whether the words used are of such a nature as to create "a clear and present danger." While the country was at war, a leaflet encouraging men to oppose the draft constituted a clear and present danger.

Abrams | The majority of the Court upheld the conviction, arguing that, although the leaflet's authors were mainly concerned with the cause of the Russian Revolution, their actions undermined the U. S. war effort by appealing to workers to stop making ammunition and by calling for a general strike during wartime. This, the majority decided, was as much a threat to the country as interfering with the military draft. Justices Holmes and Brandeis dissented, saying the circumstances did not involve a clear and present danger and that they could find no immediate evil in the leaflets.

Gitlow | The Court majority ruled to uphold the conviction, adopting what was called the "bad tendency test." Justice Sanford wrote that the state could suppress a threatened danger in its incipiency. "It cannot reasonably be required to defer the adoption of measures for its own...safety until the revolutionary utterances lead to actual disturbances of the public peace or imminent and immediate danger of its own destruction." Two justices dissented.

Terminiello | The majority ruled to reverse Terminiello's conviction, arguing that the ordinance itself was an undue restriction of free speech. The idea of free speech in a free society is to invite dispute, to challenge the listeners. It is this allowance of provocative speech which distinguishes a free society from a totalitarian society. Three justices dissented.

Tinker | The majority reversed the suspension of the students. Justice Fortas wrote that the wearing of armbands was "closely akin to 'pure speech'" and protected by the First Amendment. The school environment did imply limitations on the freedom of expression, but the principals lacked good enough reasons in this case. If it disrupted school work or school discipline it could be forbidden, but the students in this case had protested silently and passively, unaccompanied by any disorder or disturbance. The principals' fear of disturbance was insufficient. Further, other symbols expressing opinions had been allowed. Two justices dissented, arguing that the armbands had, in effect, diverted other students from their school work.

TEST QUESTIONS

Part I: Individual Skills

Identifying Evidence

Q Label each item below with the appropriate letter.

    S   A **source** of information is given.

    N   **No** source of information is given.

_____1. The ship's log of the *Half Moon* shows that Henry Hudson sailed up the Hudson River in 1609.

_____2. According to Lawrence J. Burpee in "The Fate of Henry Hudson," his crew cast Henry Hudson adrift to die in June of 1611. [*Canadian Historical Review*, XXI (December, 1940), pp. 401–6.]

_____3. Early in 1682, LaSalle and his expedition arrived at the delta of the Mississippi River and planted the French flag there.

_____4. Father Junipero Serra led an expedition in May 1769 to establish a Spanish mission at San Diego in lower California.

Evaluating Evidence

Q In the space provided, use **three** of the criteria you learned in class to evaluate the following evidence.

5. A Colonial bystander who saw the Boston Massacre said that the colonists hadn't done anything to the British soldiers who fired into the crowd. Evaluate the bystander as a source.

6. John Cooke, who is accused of stealing a valuable painting from the Gardner Museum in Boston, tells the police he can prove he didn't do it. He says that he and Bob Wilkins were together on business in Chicago all day and night on the day of the robbery. When the police call Bob, he says that he was indeed with John in Chicago on the day of the robbery. Evaluate John as a source.

Identifying Cause-and-Effect Reasoning

Q Label each item below with the appropriate letter.

    C-E The item involves **cause-and-effect reasoning**.

    N   The item does **not** involve cause-and-effect reasoning.

_____7. Columbus believed he was in the Indies near China. Consequently, he called the natives "Indians."

_____8. What explains the Spanish dominance over a huge American empire? Greed for gold and power, a sense of adventure, and the desire to Christianize the Indians kept the Spaniards exploring.

_____9. Marquette explored North America for France, just as Ponce de Leon explored for Spain.

Evaluating Cause-and-Effect Reasoning

 Use the criteria learned in class to evaluate the cause-and-effect reasoning in each of the following arguments.

10. "Our football team lost the game because our best player was injured."

Proposed cause?   *Connection?*   *Stated effect?*

Other possible causes?

Overall, how strong is this cause-and-effect reasoning? Explain your answer.

11. Jean's car stalls frequently. The mechanic who is working on the car decides that the problem can't be the starter because the car starts fine except when it is raining. The mechanic then checks the wires, discovers that one wire is cracked in two places, and concludes that this is the reason for the car's stalling.

Proposed cause?   *Connection?*   *Stated effect?*

Other possible causes?

Overall, how strong is this cause-and-effect reasoning? Explain your answer.

12. "People came to the British colonies to settle to escape religious and political persecution."

Proposed cause?   *Connection?*   *Stated effect?*

Other possible causes?

Overall, how strong is this cause-and-effect reasoning? Explain your answer.

Identifying Comparisons

 Label each item below with the appropriate letter.

    C   The item involves **comparison reasoning**.

    N   The item does **not** involve comparison reasoning.

_____ 13. We should pick Juanita for the achievement award. Peter's grades are much lower in math, and Juanita has been involved in more extracurricular activities.

_____ 14. We should keep the nuclear power plant in operation. No one has been injured there, and it provides a great deal of electricity for our area.

_____ 15. Apparently the bus went out of control when the front left tire had a blowout.

_____ 16. Countries that do not have a free press tend to be undemocratic.

_____ 17. Canada generally has a colder climate than does the United States, primarily due to its higher latitude.

Evaluating Comparisons

 Evaluate each of the following comparison arguments. Tell whether the comparison is strong or weak and explain why you think so.

18. Tom will have no trouble fixing the brakes on your bike. Last year he easily replaced my bike's chain.

19. Women before 1800 were no better off in America than they had been in Europe. They still didn't have the right to vote, and men controlled almost all the property.

20. The Constitutional Convention of 1787 brought together the best thinkers in America and produced one of history's great political documents. If we brought together today's best thinkers, we could again straighten out the government's problems.

Identifying Generalizations

 Label each item below with the appropriate letter
- **G**   The item involves **generalization reasoning**.
- **N**   The item does **not** involve generalization reasoning.

_____21. The car runs great since the engine was fixed.

_____22. Most men enjoy watching sports on TV.

_____23. Women in colonial America could not, with few exceptions, own property.

_____24. Philip took the trash out so his mother will be pleased.

_____25. Countries without a free press tend to be undemocratic.

Evaluating Generalizations

 Evaluate each of the following generalization arguments. Tell whether the generalization is strong or weak and explain why you think so.

26. A survey of 200 people at the National Democratic Convention showed that an overwhelming majority of Americans will be voting in the next election.

27. By looking at the American and French Revolutions, you can see that revolutions are caused by people seeking political freedom.

28. Of the fifty-five delegates to the Constitutional Convention, most were wealthy men or at least owned some property.

Identifying Unstated Assumptions

_____29. "The American Revolution, because it gave America independence, was more important than the French and Indian War." Which of the following is the unstated assumption in this argument?

A. The American Revolution was more important than the French and Indian War.

B. The American Revolution gave us independence from England.

C. The American Revolution was a bigger war.

D. A war that results in independence is more important than any war that does not.

30. A British government official said, "If we put a tax on sugar from the French West Indies, the colonists will buy their sugar from the British West Indies because it will be cheaper." What is the unstated assumption?

Part II: Mixed Problems

 Each of the following arguments is followed by several questions regarding that argument. In the space provided, answer each question.

> "Only 3% of the people in that country have televisions, so it must be a primitive country."

31. What is the conclusion of this argument?

32. What is the unstated assumption?

33. What word makes a value judgment?

> "The French colonies in the New World grew slowly because of the poor climate and the feudal landholding system."

_____34. What is the primary type of reasoning in this argument?

    A. Cause and Effect   B. Comparison   C. Generalization

35. Evaluate the reasoning in the above argument.

> "Riding a motorcycle without a helmet is really stupid. It's like sword fighting without a sword."

_____36. What is the primary type of reasoning in this argument?

      A. Cause and Effect   B. Comparison   C. Generalization

37.   Evaluate the reasoning.

38.   Based on the above argument, what does this person value?

Salem Witch Hysteria

 Read the following brief argument and Relevant Information regarding the Salem witch hysteria. Refer to these readings when answering questions **39–46**.

> "People have studied the Salem witch hysteria of 1692 for many years. Historians have advanced a number of theories, all of which are weak in some way. The best explanation is that the hysteria resulted primarily from the psychological makeup of Puritan society in general and Salem Village in particular. The afflicted girls were teenagers who suffered from too much control by their Calvinist (religious) society; they had no real outlets for their natural high spirits. Their accusations resulted from their anger, mainly against older women. (According to trial records, most of those accused as witches were unmarried women or widows between the ages of forty-one and sixty.) Thus, when the girls accused others of witchcraft, they were rebelling against the strict rules of the older generation. They defied the whole adult world, showing lawlessness, disobedience, and delinquency which is difficult for someone in the twentieth century to understand."

RELEVANT INFORMATION

A.   In 17th-century America, 90% of all witchcraft trials were in New England, where Calvinism was the main religion. Other religions were dominant in other parts of America.

B.   Salem Village was about five miles from Salem Town.

_____39. What is the main point of this reading?

    A. The older generation was too strict on the teenagers in Salem Village.

    B. The witch hysteria resulted mainly from the girls' boredom and their religion's control over them.

    C. The girls in Salem Village who made most of the accusations were lawless and disobedient.

    D. The adults in Salem Village never should have stood for the lawlessness and disobedience of the girls in their accusations.

_____40. How does **Relevant Information A** affect this theory?

    A. Supports it.   B. Doesn't affect it.   C. Weakens it.

_____41. How does **Relevant Information B** affect this theory?

    A. Supports it.   B. Doesn't affect it.   C. Weakens it.

_____42. Which of the following is evidence presented by the author of this argument? That is, which information in the argument includes a source?

    A. The hysteria resulted from the psychological makeup of Salem Village.

    B. The afflicted girls suffered from too much control by the Puritan society.

    C. Most of the accused witches were unmarried women or widows between the ages of forty-one and sixty.

    D. The afflicted girls defied the whole adult world.

_____43. Which of the following words in the argument makes a value judgment?

    A. Lawlessness   B. Society   C. Widowed   D. Adult world

_____44. What type of reasoning is used in sentence 3?

    A. Cause and Effect   B. Comparison   C. Generalization

_____45. The clause "most of those accused as witches were unmarried women or widowed between the ages of forty-one and sixty" is what type of reasoning?

    A. Cause and Effect   B. Comparison   C. Generalization

46. Evaluate the reasoning of the claim in question 45.

Salem Witchcraft: Viewpoints

 To refresh your memory, each historian's main point is given below. For each, read that the sentence starts "The main cause of the Salem Witch Trials was... ."

Historian A	...clergymen.	Historian E	...belief in and practice of witchcraft.
Historian B	...disputes between neighbors.	Historian F	...community picking on social outcasts.
Historian C	...girls' boredom.	Historian G	...conditions in 1692.
Historian D	...ergot poisoning.	Historian H	...political divisions within Salem Village.

How would each piece of information affect the viewpoints that follow it? Write the letter of your choice in the blank provided.

"In an epidemic in Finland, 56% of the people with ergotism were under ten years of age. In another epidemic 60% were under fifteen years of age. In Salem three of the eleven girls were under fifteen and one was under ten years of age. There was one other case in Salem of a child under ten years of age with the symptoms of ergotism. It was an eight-week-old infant who was nursing, so would not have eaten rye bread."

_____47. This evidence:

    A. Provides major support for Historian D

    B. Provides minor support for Historian D

    C. Does not affect Historian D

    D. Mildly weakens Historian D

    E. Significantly weakens Historian D

"In Bridget Bishop's examination for witchcraft, two men testified that they had found puppets commonly used for witchcraft in her home."

_____48. This evidence:

    A. Supports Historian A

    B. Supports Historian E

    C. Weakens Historian G

    D. Weakens Historian C

    E. Supports Historian D

"Reverend Samuel Parris preached several sermons in 1692 on the Devil. On March 27, 1692, he said, 'Christ knows how many devils (are) among us....' On September 11, 1692, he said, 'There are no neuters (neutrals). Everyone is on one side or the other.... It calls on us all...to mourn that the devil has had so many assistants from amongst us.' "

_____49. This evidence:

    A. Weakens Historian H

    B. Supports Historian G

    C. Supports Historian C

    D. Supports Historian A

    E. Weakens Historian C

"One of the persons accused of witchcraft was Sarah Good, a beggar. Many of the people in Salem Village did not like her."

_____50. This evidence:

    A. Supports Historian E

    B. Supports Historian F

    C. Weakens Historian F

    D. Supports Historian G

    E. Weakens Historian G

TEST SOLUTION SUGGESTIONS

Explanation

As mentioned in the introduction, students should be evaluated in a variety of ways, not just by objective tests. So, although fifty test items are included in the *Teacher's Guide*, you should also consider evaluating students using problems from the student text. One of the best evaluation methods is to give students one interpretation you haven't analyzed in class and have them write an evaluation of it. You could supply the criteria for evaluation, such as finding the main idea, identifying and evaluating two pieces of evidence, identifying and evaluating two types of reasoning, identifying one assumption, bringing in any relevant information on the topic, and making an overall judgment.

The fifty items on the test are meant to examine student mastery of the skills listed on the scope and sequence chart on pages 10–11, primarily identifying and evaluating evidence, cause-and-effect reasoning, comparison reasoning, generalization reasoning, and identifying unstated assumptions. There are also some test questions on using relevant information, finding the main idea, and identifying words which make value judgments (analyzing language). Identifying and evaluating proof reasoning and evaluating ethical claims are not tested since there are no specific lessons on these skills in the student book.

Suggested Answers

**Part I:
Individual Skills**

IDENTIFYING EVIDENCE

1. S The ship's log is the source.
2. S The article is the source.
3. N
4. N

EVALUATING EVIDENCE

5. Strength: Primary source.

   Weaknesses: The colonist has a reason to lie; no other evidence verifies what this person says.

6. Strengths: Primary source; Bob Wilkens verifies his story.

   Weakness: John has a reason to lie.

IDENTIFYING CAUSE-AND-EFFECT REASONING

7. C-E
8. C-E
9. N

EVALUATING CAUSE-AND-EFFECT REASONING

10. Proposed Cause: Best player injured.

    Connection: Reasonable.

    Stated Effect: We lost.

    Other possible causes: Other team was better; we were outplayed.

    Overall, although this analysis shows that not having the best player could have been the main reason for the loss, other causes are just as likely. The arguer should have discussed these.

11. There is a reasonable connection between a car having cracked wires (Proposed Cause) and stalling (Stated Effect). Moreover, the mechanic eliminated another possible cause (starter). Students might decide that these are the only two possible causes (so the reasoning is strong), or they might think there are other possible causes which should have been considered (so the reasoning is weak). Either conclusion is acceptable; it's the thinking (mentioning other causes) that is important.

12. Since the argument doesn't consider other possible reasons (economic and personal, for example) for coming to the British colonies, the reasoning is weak.

IDENTIFYING COMPARISONS

13. C
14. N
15. N
16. N It doesn't compare democratic to undemocratic countries.
17. C

EVALUATING COMPARISON REASONING

18. This is a weak comparison, since fixing brakes is very different from replacing a chain.

19. This is a weak comparison; women may have been much better off in other ways such as standard of living, political rights other than voting, and social freedoms.

20. This is a weak comparison since the conditions and problems today are very different from those in 1787 (and the quality of today's best thinkers may not be as good as it was in 1787).

IDENTIFYING GENERALIZATIONS

21. N
22. G
23. G
24. N
25. G

EVALUATING GENERALIZATIONS

26. This generalization is weak. Because people who attend political conventions tend to vote much more frequently than the general public, the sample does not represent all qualified voters well.

27. This is a weak generalization because the sample is too small (only two revolutions). It also does not represent twentieth century revolutions well.

28. This is a strong generalization because the whole group was probably examined.

IDENTIFYING UNSTATED ASSUMPTIONS

29. D

30. There are several. Colonists base their decisions about buying sugar mainly on price; colonists can't get around the tax (i.e., by smuggling); British and French West Indies are the only places colonists can get sugar; colonists will continue to buy sugar.

Part II:
Mixed Problems
(PRIMITIVE COUNTRY)

31. Conclusion: It must be a primitive country.
32. Assumption: People who don't have televisions are primitive (or people who are not primitive have televisions).
33. Value judgment: "primitive"

(FRENCH COLONIES)

34. A
35. Although two reasonable causes are suggested, the author does not connect them to the conclusion. Also, there are other possible causes, such as political decisions, for the slow growth.

(MOTORCYCLE)

36. B
37. The two cases are similar in that they both involve danger and equipment. They are different in that a helmet protects one directly while a sword inflicts harm on another and thus protects indirectly. A sword fighter without a sword is much more likely to be injured than a motorcyclist without a helmet.
38. This person values safety.

SALEM WITCH HYSTERIA

39. B
40. A It supports the idea that strictness (Calvinists were strict) caused the trials.
41. B
42. C
43. A
44. A
45. C "Most" is the key word.
46. The sample is probably complete, so the claim that most of the accused were unmarried or widowed is probably true. It's a strong generalization.

SALEM WITCHCRAFT: VIEWPOINTS

47. D/E It shows that the Salem girls did not fit the correct ages for outbreaks of ergotism.
48. B
49. D
50. B

Notes:

Notes:

Notes:

Notes:

Notes:

Notes: